Godet we
Goodwin
to FPL

THE
MAGINOT LINE

Myth and Reality

Nations who possess a fine army have no need
of fortresses . . . but fortresses without a
fine army have no value for defence.

Machiavelli, *The Art of War*

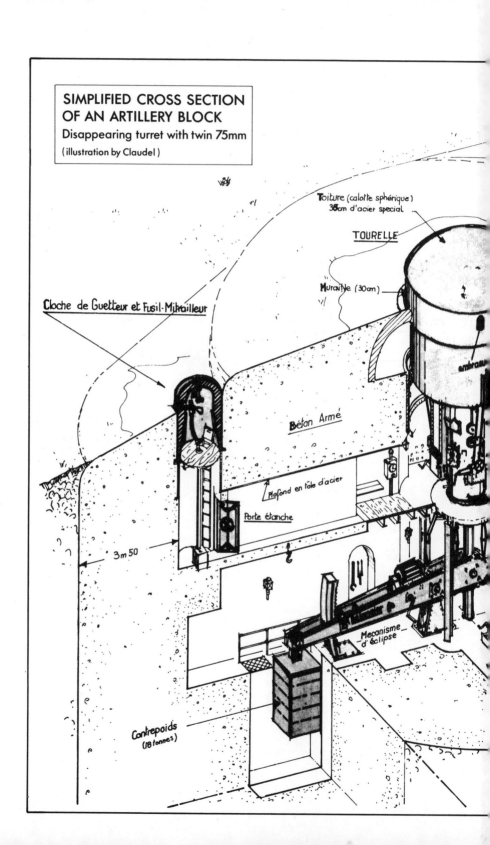

SIMPLIFIED CROSS SECTION OF AN ARTILLERY BLOCK
Disappearing turret with twin 75mm
(illustration by Claudel)

Toiture (calotte sphérique)
35cm d'acier special

TOURELLE

Muraille (30cm)

Cloche de Guetteur et Fusil-Mitrailleur

Béton Armé

Plafond en tôle d'acier

Porte étanche

3m 50

Mecanisme d'éclipse

Contrepoids
(18 tonnes)

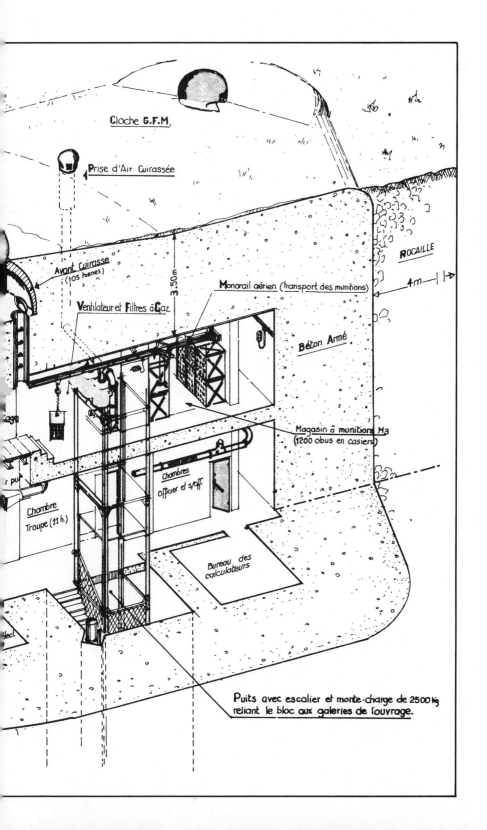

Cloche G.F.M.

← Prise d'Air Cuirassée

ROCAILLE

Avant Cuirasse
(105 tonnes)

3.50 m

4m

Ventilateur et Filtres à Gaz

Monorail aérien (transport des munitions)

Béton Armé

Magasin à munitions M3
(1200 obus en casiers)

Chambres
Officier et s/off.

Chambre
Troupe (11 h.)

Bureau des
calculateurs

Puits avec escalier et monte-charge de 2500 kg
reliant le bloc aux galeries de l'ouvrage.

Also by Anthony Kemp
The Unknown Battle: Metz, 1944

THE
MAGINOT LINE

Myth and Reality

Anthony Kemp

STEIN AND DAY/*Publishers*/New York

First published in the United States of America in 1982
Copyright © 1982 by Anthony Kemp
All rights reserved
Printed in the United States of America
Stein and Day/*Publishers*
Scarborough House
Briarcliff Manor, New York 10510

Library of Congress Cataloging in Publication Data

Kemp, Anthony.
· The Maginot Line.

  Originally published: London : F. Warne, 1981.
  Bibliography: p.
  Includes index.
  1. Maginot Line. 2. World War, 1939-1945 - Campaigns
- France. 3. France - History - German occupation, 1940-
1945. I. Title.
D761.K38 1981   940.54'21   806260
ISBN 0-8128-2811-9   AACR2

Contents

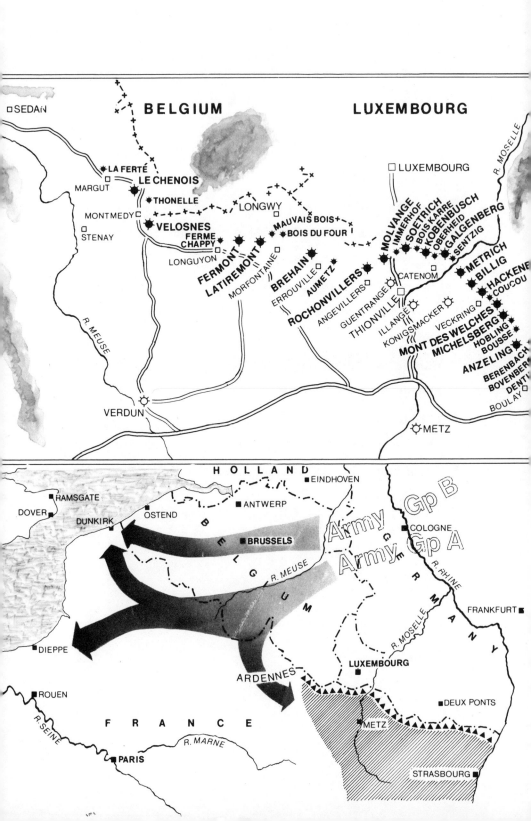

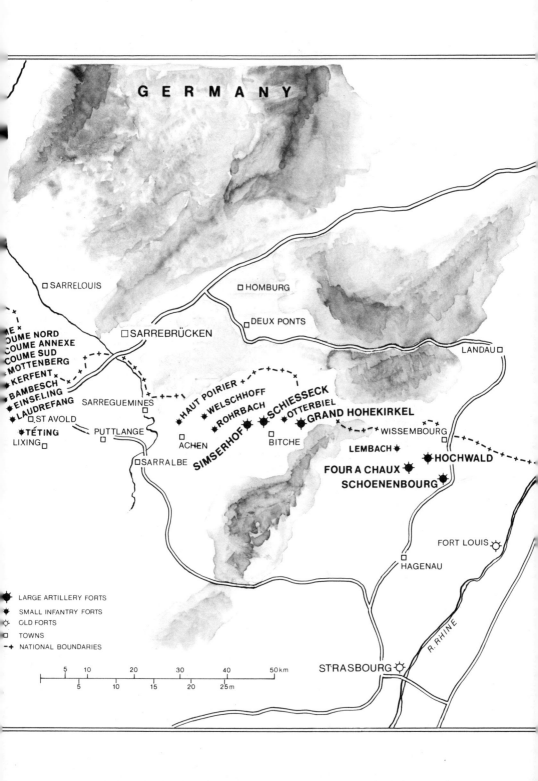

G E R M A N Y

□ SARRELOUIS

□ HOMBURG

□ DEUX PONTS

ME ×
OUME NORD
COUME ANNEXE
COUME SUD
MOTTENBERG
♦ KERFENT ×
BAMBESCH
EINSELING
♦ LAUDREFANG
□ ST AVOLD
♦ TÉTING
LIXING□

□ SARREBRÜCKEN

LANDAU □

SARREGUEMINES
□

♦ HAUT POIRIER
♦ WELSCHHOFF
♦ ROHRBACH   ♦ SCHIESSECK
PUTTLANGE   SIMSERHOF ♦ ♦ ♦ OTTERBIEL
□   ACHEN   BITCHE   ♦ GRAND HOHEKIRKEL
□ SARRALBE   WISSEMBOURG □

LEMBACH ♦
FOUR A CHAUX ♦
SCHOENENBOURG ♦ ♦ HOCHWALD

FORT LOUIS ☼

□ HAGENAU

♦ LARGE ARTILLERY FORTS
♦ SMALL INFANTRY FORTS
☼ OLD FORTS
□ TOWNS
–+ NATIONAL BOUNDARIES

R. RHINE

STRASBOURG ☼

5   10   20   30   40   50km
|___|___|____|____|____|____|
  5   10   15   20   25m

Acknowledgements

I owe a very great debt to the *Association Saint-Maurice pour la recherche de documents sur la forteresse,* and their president, Major Jean-Jacques Rapin. Thanks to his kindness and generosity, I have been able to study books and pamphlets otherwise unobtainable in this country. In addition, the Association kindly gave me permission to reproduce certain drawings and photographs of which they own the copyright. Many other people have helped in various ways. Phillipe Truttman has corresponded with me over a number of years and gave me the benefit of his vast knowledge of the subject. Messrs Beyer and Heymès of *Amifort* provided me with details of the parts of the Line open to the public and obtained certain booklets for me. Dennis Quarmby spent a large amount of his time copying photographs, and Ian Hogg provided essential information. Victor Smith scoured London for some photocopies of articles that I needed in a hurry, and Lieut-Commander C. B. Robbins USN sent me some interesting maps. Miss Susan Lemke, John Goodwin and Herbert Jäger kindly loaned me books. Général Robert Nicolas gave me the benefit of his extensive technical knowledge and produced a book otherwise unobtainable in this country. Finally, Eversley Belfield gave me a shove in the right direction. The above, many of whom are fellow members of the Fortress Study Group, provided the technical back-up. On a personal note, my wife has had to endure uncomfortable holidays spent in search of the Maginot Line, and my thanks are due to her patience and forbearance.

Introduction

Ever since prehistoric times man has been engaged in improving the defensive capabilities of his environment, either to defend his property from predators or to secure his own base while attacking his neighbours. This logical activity is known as fortification, which can be defined as: creating an obstacle between one's own position and a potential enemy, or improving upon an existing natural one. As an art or science it is today more or less obsolete, as aircraft can overfly man-made defences and bomb the object to be protected.

With the exception of the Great Wall of China, the Maginot Line was the greatest system of permanent fortification ever built, and probably the last. In spite of this, it has remained relatively unknown as far as its technical construction and history are concerned. What is known about it is its unenviable reputation for being the greatest White Elephant of all times.

Many writers, trying to justify a point of military futility, have seized upon the Maginot Line as being the classic example, which is to ignore the fact that the defences fulfilled the purpose for which they were constructed—to stop a German invasion of Alsace and Lorraine. The fact that they decided to invade elsewhere is another matter. The Line has even been blamed for the fall of France in 1940. The latter, however, was caused by a mixture of moral and political degeneration and the blindness of the military authorities to the development of warfare after 1918.

The reality of the Maginot Line remains as a monument to man's technical ingenuity, and, as an inanimate object, cannot be held responsible for the blindness of its creators. There were, however, two lines: the real one and the propaganda one. It is the latter which represents the myth.

I use the term 'Maginot Line' throughout this book as this is the name popularly associated with the pre-1940 French frontier defences. The title, however, was a figment of media imagination, coined in the 1930s to simplify abstruse military terminology.

André Maginot was a politician who, among other things, secured the necessary funds from an unwilling Chamber of Deputies to build the defences. It is one of the injustices of history that his name has been unfairly coupled with something for which he was not technically responsible and which was mainly built after his death.

The many excellent studies of the Battle of France in 1940 all mention the Maginot Line, but only in passing and without going into any detail. Informed literature in English is non-existent. Anything written before the war was largely inspired by propaganda motives or based on 'official' hand-outs. Only during the last few years have a number of books, limited-circulation treatises and articles in military journals appeared on the Continent.

It is only fairly recently that public interest in the subject has been awakened. Several of the forts have been restored and can be visited. French official circles, however, remain silent, and the Maginot Line is still a military secret—at least in theory.

This book is a synthesis of the available evidence from both primary and secondary sources and an attempt to do justice to a fine piece of engineering. It is not an exhaustive treatise (for which there is insufficient evidence available), but is designed to help those who are interested in the period to understand the significance of the French fortifications. Apart from the pure technicalities, it is necessary to place the Maginot Line in its correct historical perspective. This I hope I have achieved.

Chapter 1

The situation of France
in 1918

Political

The French won World War I—or so they thought. In 1918, after four years of bitter conflict, the nation erupted in joyful celebration. The arch-enemy, Germany, had been defeated and the lost provinces of Alsace and Lorraine had been reunited with the homeland. The humiliation of 1870 had been avenged and, on the surface at least, France was the most powerful nation in Europe. Germany was prostrate, its autocratic monarchy tumbled and the country rent by internal dissention.

The reality was different. The northern provinces, as a result of the fighting, had been totally devastated and depopulated. The treasury was empty and saddled with a vast burden of war debt. The French diplomat, Jules Cambon, wrote prophetically at the time, 'France victorious must grow accustomed to being a lesser power than France vanquished'.

The paradox was that Germany had emerged from the war far stronger. France had a static population of some 40 million, but was confronted by 70 million Germans whose territory had not been ravaged and who had a higher birth-rate. The Austro-Hungarian Empire had been split up into a number of smaller units, none of which could pose a serious threat to Germany. Russia, once the pillar of the Triple-Entente, forcing Germany to fight on two fronts, had dissolved into internal chaos. The recreation of an independent Poland after the war produced a barrier between Russia and Germany which meant that the old ally of France no longer directly threatened German territory.

Like their predecessors a century earlier at Vienna, the statesmen gathered at Versailles in 1919 to redraw the map of Europe. There was a general cry of 'Germany must pay', but what the French desired above all was security. She no longer had any territorial claims against the erstwhile enemy, but demanded viable frontiers and international guarantees. Her eyes were fixed firmly on the Rhineland. Foch, the Allied generalissimo, demanded that the German frontier be the east bank of the Rhine, with the French army permanently based on the west bank, where the German population was to be formed into an autonomous state dominated by France. As Woodrow Wilson, the President of the United States, sensibly observed, Foch and his supporters were simply trying to create another Alsace–Lorraine. This type of problem has been well illustrated in recent years by the Israeli occupation of Arab territory after the Six-Day War.

What the French did gain at Versailles was the right to occupy the Rhineland until 1936, although, at the Treaty of Locarno in 1925, this date was brought forward to 1930. The disputed frontier province of the Saarland was to be administered by France on behalf of the League of Nations until a plebiscite determined its future nationality. The fate of this latter area was to have an important bearing on the subsequent decisions concerning the siting of the Maginot Line.

For France, however, the main aim of the peace was to ensure that Germany would no longer be in a position to threaten that security which she so ardently desired. Thus Germany was to be disarmed, her armed forces reduced to a cadre of 100,000 men and her fortresses demolished. The entire west bank of the Rhine was to be demilitarized to a depth of 50 miles, to create an additional buffer to future aggression, behind which France could feel safe.

With the benefit of hindsight we can now see that the Treaty of Versailles was a patched-up peace that left Germany in a strong position and with a deep desire to overturn the settlement. During the negotiations it became apparent that France was harbouring a dangerous illusion, namely that her allies during the war would always come to her aid if she were again threatened by Germany. As the idealism of the peace gradually ebbed away, so the Anglo-Saxon nations slid deeper and deeper into isolationism, busy with their own post-war problems. In Britain there was a strong feeling that Germany had been too harshly treated, coupled with suspicions of French motives over such questions as that of the Saarland. Another illusion was that France alone had been responsible for the victory. Both Britain and America knew this to be untrue, and soon came to hold the view that their sacrifice had not been worth the achievement of regaining Alsace and Lorraine for an ungrateful France.[1]

Military

While the statesmen were hammering out the peace terms, which left Germany intact as a nation, the French military authorities were making their own assessments of the situation. It has been said that the inspiration for the Maginot Line is to be found in the military cemeteries of northern France and Flanders, which is to a large extent true. The French army was faced by a demographic problem which it was unable to solve in the short or medium term. They discovered that between 1914 and 1918 France had lost some 1.4 million men killed, plus 4.3 million wounded more or less seriously, and 500,000 missing. The figures on their own were bad enough, but reach their full significance when quoted as a percentage of the total mobilized—73 per cent. One more such war and France would be finished as a nation. The figures showed that in 1934 there would be a sudden drop in the number of conscripts available, which would reach a peak in 1938/9, before a new generation came of age for military service. All this meant that, whatever strategy France chose to adopt, it would have to be based on conservation of manpower.

Another fact that was immediately apparent was that the French frontier defences no longer corresponded to the political realities. Traditionally France had always based her defences on fixed fortifications, producing in the process some of the greatest military engineers. Indeed, French was the international language of fortification, and generations of cadets at the military academies had been brought up on the systems of Vauban and Cormontaigne.

After the loss to Germany of Alsace and Lorraine in 1870, which included the fortresses of Strasbourg, Metz and Thionville, the German frontier had been advanced to within 250 km of Paris. To counter this, a new scheme of defence was proposed by the engineer General Séré de Rivières.[2] His aim was to create an artificial barrier between the North Sea and the Mediterranean. For economic reasons the only part of this scheme to be fully realized was that which covered the new north-eastern frontier. Two fortified zones were built, between Verdun and Toul, and Épinal and Belfort, using the natural advantages of the heights of the Meuse and the Moselle respectively. These zones would, in theory, hold up any German attack while the main army was mobilized and deployed.

By 1919 these works were far back from the new border, leaving Alsace and Lorraine defenceless. Apart from this, the regained provinces housed an important industrial area along the Moselle valley which it was vital to deny to a German attacker. Thus it was clear to the authorities right from the start that some form of defensive programme would have to be undertaken.

So, although on paper in 1918 the French army was the most powerful in the world, with all the prestige of victory, there were many problems to be overcome, both demographic and geographic. It is an old adage that generals always fight the last war, especially if they have won it. The French settled down to plan for the next conflict along already proven lines, encumbered with a vast quantity of outdated equipment. By forcing the Germans to disarm, they ensured that in any future conflict, the former enemy would be better armed.

Chapter 2

The decisions that led to the Maginot Line

At the end of World War I the French army was split into two schools of thought—the offensive and the defensive. The former was led by Marshal Foch. Before the war, as an instructor at the *École Supérieure de la Guerre*, he had preached the paramount virtue of the offensive regardless of circumstances. He and his supporters believed that French *élan* would carry her armies to victory, a belief that was to have tragic consequences during the early battles of 1914. The French *poilus*, still dressed in their traditional red pantaloons, charged to their death in thousands, mown down by the invincible machine-guns. During the subsequent stalemate, commanders on both sides naturally dreamed of the offensive movement that would break the barrier of trenches.

In 1918, Foch, as commander of the victorious allied armies, still believed in the offensive spirit and in Napoleon's edict that 'It is an axiom of war that the side which stays within its fortifications is beaten'. His answer to the problem of French security, if threatened by Germany, was an immediate offensive across the Rhine.

However, other councils prevailed and responsible military circles were convinced that France could not afford another blood-letting. Looking back to the recent experience of trench warfare, the staff officers realized the cost in manpower of offensive action. Would not the defensive be a better answer to their problems? They persuaded themselves that, as the line of trenches had held, and that, in spite of this, they had won the war, it must be the best form of strategy. If they entrenched themselves behind some form of permanent defences, a German onslaught could be held until such time as France's allies could come to her aid and their blockade take effect. Replacing the comparatively unsophisticated trench systems with powerful forts built in peacetime as a precaution would provide the shield that they sought.

Verdun was in many ways the key factor responsible for the growth of defensive thinking. The 10-month battle there in 1916 had been a purely French effort, and almost every soldier who had survived the war had served there at some time or another. The old city and its battlefields became endowed with a semi-mystical character as a place of pilgrimage between the wars which endures to a certain extent even today. The emotive phrase coined by Pétain, *'Ils ne passeront pas'*, was to be adopted by the Maginot Line garrisons as their motto, altered from plural to singular.

The French believed that Verdun had demonstrated that a continuous line of trenches could be held against any odds, and therefore that such a strategy must be sound. This hypothesis was certainly true as far as Verdun was concerned, but what they conveniently forgot was that in the spring of 1918 the Germans managed to break through the lines. Instead of solid lines of riflemen advancing shoulder to shoulder across no-man's land, preceded by a shattering bombardment that announced their coming, the Germans used small groups of skirmishers who operated flexibly. Armed with light portable weapons, they probed for weak spots in the defences and left strongpoints to be mopped up later. Another factor overlooked was the development of efficient tanks, which, by 1918, had already proved their value in mobile warfare. In this respect, however, one cannot only blame the French for blindness. The other European nations, once the war was over, tended to dismiss such 'freaks' as armour and aircraft, and to return happily to peacetime soldiering. The German General Staff showed no interest in tanks. Guderian was given the chance to develop the *panzer* division by Hitler's political movement, not by his military superiors.

In addition to the trench system, Verdun also demonstrated the value of permanent fortifications. The city had been surrounded by a ring of forts as part of the post-1870 programme, and when the high-explosive shell appeared during the 1880s, a number of them were modified. Layers of concrete were added on top and the guns were placed in armoured turrets. During the initial stages of the German offensive in 1914 the Belgian forts at Liège and Namur, of similar date to those at Verdun, were pulverized by heavy artillery. As a result, it was decided to disarm the French forts wherever possible and use the guns as reinforcements for the field army. When the Battle of Verdun started in

1916 the forts were naturally bombarded by the Germans, as they were still in use as troop shelters. Much to the surprise of the French generals, the supposedly outdated works proved capable of withstanding the impact of shells of up to 42 cm calibre. The reason for this was, that instead of being constructed of a solid block of concrete like the Belgian ones, the modified French forts had two layers of concrete with sand in between. Impacting shells tended to burst on the outer skin and expend their energy into the air instead of penetrating. As a result, the forts were rapidly rearmed and played a useful part in the battle.[3]

After the war there was no immediate hurry; the German forces had been disarmed and the French army occupied the Rhineland. It was not until May 1920, that a commission was appointed to study the nature of the country's frontier defences, under the presidency of the ageing Marshal Joffre, the victor of the Marne. Following the obligatory visit to Verdun, where he was duly impressed by the relatively undamaged forts, he and his supporters came to the conclusion that the answer to French security lay in the construction of a number of powerful fortified zones between the North Sea and the Alps. Shielded by these, the field armies could mobilize and await the favourable moment to attack. This viewpoint was embodied in a report presented in 1920, entitled *Note on the General Organisation of National Territory*.[4]

In 1921, however, Marshal Pétain launched a counter-attack. He had been appointed Inspector-General of the Army and, as such, was the Commander-in-Chief designate in the event of hostilities. His report is of great interest because it formed the basis of French strategic doctrine right up to 1940. He was convinced that the answer lay in what he described as 'battlefields prepared in peacetime', by which he understood a continuous front on the principle of the wartime trenches. What is interesting is that he foresaw these only for the length of the western frontier along the Rhine, and from there to Thionville on the Moselle. As far as the rest of the frontier was concerned, 'It can only be defended from inside Belgium'. We will discuss the geographic and strategic implications of this later, but must first examine the role played by Pétain himself.

Henri Philippe Pétain was born in 1856 and entered St Cyr in 1876. His promotion was slow and his career undistinguished. But for the outbreak of war he would have faded into genteel oblivion. Joffre, however, remembered the instructor at the *École de Guerre* who had specialized in infantry tactics, and appointed Pétain to his staff in 1914. Thence he gravitated to command an army, becoming celebrated as the saviour of Verdun and the man who dealt with the 1917 mutinies. His weakness was that his military intellect became frozen after Verdun, characterized by pessimism, suspicion of the British and a total inability to take any form of risk.

Nevertheless, after the war his prestige was enormous. He was the man who had saved France and who had the interests of the common soldier at heart. It is no use blaming him for strapping the French army into an intellectual strait-jacket; they donned it willingly, backed by the weight of public opinion and sentiment. All over Europe it was believed that the age of universal peace and disarmament had dawned.

The discussion raged throughout the early 1920s. From 1922 to 1925 the *Commission Speciale de Défense du Territoire* concerned itself with the problem, before being superseded by the *Commission de Défense des Frontières*, presided over by General Guillaumat.[5] As their titles suggest, the various commissions were dedicated solely to the discussion of defence. No considerations of alternative strategy were allowed to intrude. The problem was what sort of defences and where to build them. The protagonists of the Pétain school argued that the flimsy trenches had withstood the most furious bombardments, while the supporters of the Joffre school justly claimed that the Allies had finally advanced through the German Hindenburg Line. All this controversy was carried out in an unhurried atmosphere, although Germany was already busily circumventing the military provisions of the Treaty of Versailles.

France had extensive land frontiers to defend, all of which had to be considered by the various commissions. Historically there have been four classic invasion routes into the country: across the Flanders plain; down the valley of the Moselle; the Belfort Gap between the Vosges and the Alps; and along the Riviera. The Riviera route had never been successful, but, as we shall see, the basic proposals that led to what became known as the Maginot Line took into account the other three.

The eastern frontier of France runs along the Rhine from the Swiss border at Basle to Lauterbourg, a distance of some 150 km. The river itself is a good natural barrier and for part of its length it is backed by a canal running parallel to it. Further in the rear are the Vosges mountains which cover the entire frontier except for the famous gap at the south end, blocked by the fortress of Belfort. The mountains are difficult to penetrate and the few east–west roads run in deep ravines. If the Belfort Gap were blocked by powerful modern fortifications, the rest of the eastern frontier could be guarded by road-blocks and pillboxes. At least, that was the theory.

To the north the common frontier with Germany leaves the Rhine at Lauterbourg and runs north-west until it reaches Luxembourg. The landscape is characterized by rolling and often wooded hills crossed by several rivers, the most important of which is the Moselle. Although not ideal country for mobile warfare, this area was successfully exploited by the Germans in 1870. The actual border is difficult to defend, being virtually devoid of natural obstacles capable of improvement. The logical step would have been to base the defences further in the rear, which would have had the added advantage of shortening the line considerably—the shorter the line the less troops you require to defend it. Ideally, the fortifications could have been built to link the Meuse and Moselle valleys from Sedan to Metz, continuing on to meet the Vosges at Sarrebourg. The post-1870 French defences were not anchored to a political frontier, but used strong natural positions—the initial defence was to be carried out by strong bodies of troops operating in front of them. However, in the light of economic factors that have come to dominate modern warfare, it was logistically impossible to abandon the vital industrial areas of the Briey iron-ore deposits and the Moselle valley.

West of the Moselle, the frontier area becomes more hilly along the Luxembourg border, which leads into the area known as the Ardennes. Much has been written about the lack of defence of the Ardennes in 1940. However, in the knowledge that French strategic thought between the wars was based on the premise of position warfare, it is not surprising that the area was considered unsuitable for the operation of armies. To leap ahead for a moment to March 1934, when Pétain was War Minister, he appeared before the Senate Army Commission to answer questions concerned with the fortification of the Belgian frontier. Weygand and Gamelin, the senior army generals, had asked for money to build defences there, a step that was opposed by Pétain. On that occasion he made the following reply to questions about the Ardennes:

It is impenetrable if one makes some special dispositions there. Consequently we consider it a zone of destructions. Naturally the edges on the enemy side will be protected. Some blockhouses will be installed. As this front would not have any depth the enemy would not commit himself there. If he does we will pinch him off as he emerges from the forests. This sector is not dangerous.[6]

This must surely rank among the all-time classics of famous last words, in view of the events at Sedan six years later. However, one cannot load all the blame onto the shoulders of the elderly marshal. There was no storm of protest at his words and the bulk of the army agreed with him. The problem was that the 'special dispositions' were not implemented.

From the Ardennes to the North Sea the rest of the common frontier with Belgium is fairly low-lying, again with no obvious natural defensive line. When the idea of the Maginot Line was first discussed, Belgium, under the leadership of King Albert I, had a strong defensive alliance with France. This was based on the assumption that French troops would advance into that country if it were attacked by Germany. This was Pétain's doctrine and thus became a cardinal point of French strategy. Belgium had a strong line of fortifications based on the line of the River Meuse and then back along the Albert Canal to Antwerp. The original scope of the Maginot Line, as we shall see, was designed to link up with these Belgian works. Had political considerations not intervened after construction had begun, which will be discussed in a later chapter, the Germans might well have been confronted by 'a wall of steel and concrete from the North Sea to the Alps'.

Apart from purely military considerations, the whole problem of fortifying the frontier to the north-west of the Ardennes was vexed by geographic, economic and political considerations. In view of the alliance with Belgium, how could France morally justify the fortification of their common frontier without giving the impression that, when danger threatened, she would not advance to help? Besides, it would imply lack of confidence in the Belgian army. In September 1928, Paul Painlevé, who was André Maginot's successor as War Minister, stated, 'The fortification of the Belgian frontier will be less important, because we cannot build up impregnable defences in the faces of our friends the Belgians'.

Apart from the above political considerations, however, even if France had wanted to fortify the frontier from the Ardennes to the North Sea, complicated constructions of the type which were to become the integral part of the Maginot Line would have been impossible. The whole of the Flanders plain is so low-lying that observation from commanding heights would have been impossible to achieve. In addition, any attempt to construct underground forts would have resulted in rapid flooding of the sites.

A further complication was that northern France harbours the vast industrial area of Lille–Turcoign–Roubaix which rambles across the Belgian frontier towards Mons. To fortify this sector would have involved a wholesale demolition of valuable property in order to obtain adequate fields of fire, and even then, no real depth would have been achieved. Thus, any defences would have had to be sited well to the rear of the urban area, an economic impossibility. Such a key industrial complex could not be abandoned for the enemy to exploit, as the Germans had been able to do from 1914 to 1918.

In view of the above, Pétain was correct in his belief that the only way to defend northern France was to advance into Belgium. However, to protect such a huge area meant a large army, which placed France in a quandary owing to her lack of manpower, to obviate which the idea of building fortifications had been proposed in the first place. Besides, her entire security in the north rested on the arrangements and good will of a neighbouring state too weak to defend herself.

Between theory and practice there is often a wide gulf. The above geographical considerations were all obvious to the various defence committees, and a case could be made for a number of ideal solutions. The final result, however, was naturally enough a compromise, dictated largely by financial considerations.

It is at this stage in our survey of the factors that led up to the final decision to create the Maginot Line that a few words should be said about André Maginot himself and the contribution that he made to the earlier history of the work that bore his name. Before the 1914–18 war he had been a minor politician, whose family originated from Lorraine— hence his abiding interest in the protection of his ancestral homeland. Waiving his parliamentary immunity, he enlisted into the army at the outbreak of hostilities, rose to the rank of sergeant and was severely wounded. Upon recovering, he returned to politics, serving for a while as Minister for Colonies. He was a rarity among French politicians of that period in that he was honest and straightforward; even his many enemies acknowledged his integrity. He also possessed the ability to judge the realities of a situation, refusing to take refuge in the cloud-cuckoo-land of self-delusion that France indulged in after 1918.

His great fear was for an unsatisfactory peace, and his vision saw through the illusion of security created at Versailles. A speech he made at the time ran partly as follows:

We are always the invaded, we are always the ones who suffer, we are always the ones to be sacrificed. [Here he was ignoring the depredations of Louis XIV, the

French Revolutionary and Napoleonic wars.] Fifteen invasions in less than six centuries give us the right to insist on a victor's treaty that will offer us something more realistic than temporary solutions and hopes ... This treaty does not provide certainties, either in respect of the reparations due to us, or in respect of security.

These prophetic words underline his later preoccupation with national defence. Initially, however, he poured his vast energy into the matter of just compensation for the victims of the war. As Minister of Pensions in the Millerand government, his personality, backed by his own experiences, succeeded in overcoming bureaucratic inertia. Himself working long hours and forcing his staff to do likewise, he succeeded in securing pension rights for literally thousands of veterans who might otherwise have had to wait for years. When Poincaré offered him the War Ministry in 1922 there was such a public outcry that he continued to run the Ministry of Pensions in addition to his new duties.

As War Minister he became directly involved in the defence controversy, and did all he could to prod the lumbering commissions into action. It was probably as a result of his background influence that by 1926 (he himself was replaced as Minister in 1924, but contined as President of the Parliamentary Army Committee) a compromise was reached between the two rival schools of thought. This foresaw the following solutions for the frontiers of the north and north-east, and the proposals form the basis for what later became known as the Maginot Line.[7]

The frontier from the North Sea to Hirson (where the Ardennes start) would be protected by field fortifications which would only be activated in time of war (Pétain's prepared battlefield). From Hirson to Longuyon, the Ardennes sector would be defended by a dense zone of demolitions—also only to be activated on mobilization. Again this latter proposal was pure Pétain.

The rest of the frontier with Germany, and thus directly threatened, would be protected by three fortified zones, based on the powerful forts proposed by Joffre and his followers:

1   The Metz fortified region, between Longuyon and Téting (on the River Nied), designed to block off the Moselle Valley and to protect the Briey–Thionville industrial area.
2   The Lauter fortified region, between the rivers Saar and Rhine, to block the route taken by the Germans in 1870.
3   The Upper Alsace fortified region, between the Vosges and the

Swiss border, designed to block the Belfort Gap. (This latter section was never implemented due to lack of funds.)

Thus, eight years after the end of the war, we have the initial statement of principle. The works were planned to cope with three of the four traditional invasion routes previously mentioned. Once the politicians and strategists had made up their minds what was required, the matter was referred to other hands for practical implementation. Indeed, once the decision to build forts was finally made, the work was carried out with surprising rapidity. However, political and strategic considerations were to continue to dog the works known as the Maginot Line.

Chapter 3

The Maginot Line in theory and practice

Having decided to stake their security on permanent defences, the French authorities proceeded initially with a certain amount of vigour, spurred on by the imminent withdrawal from the Rhineland. However, before looking at the actual construction of the works in detail, it is well to examine the theoretical background. The purpose of the fortifications was as follows:

Firstly, to protect the frontiers against a surprise attack, delivered without prior declaration of war. In French literature of the period this was known as an *attaque brusquée*, which had been examined as a theoretical possibility in certain articles written by General von Seekt, the head of the German *Reichswehr*. Seekt's premise was that Germany's only chance was to strike before blockade and the mobilization of Anglo-American forces could take effect. Germany at the time did not have the means to carry out such an attack, but the threat was taken seriously nonetheless.

Secondly, in case of a formal declaration of war, to protect the frontiers during the vital three weeks needed for mobilization. The key word here is the *couverture* which would be provided by the fortifications and their garrisons. This 'cover' would consist of regular army units plus some reserves and the annual class of conscripts, based on the fortifications. It was a step short of full mobilization but could be activated rapidly if danger threatened.[8]

Thirdly, after mobilization had been completed, to provide a core for resistance and to ensure the integrity of the nation and its industrial potential.

Since France no longer had any territorial claims against Germany, no serious thoughts about using the fortifications as a base for an offensive seem to have been entertained, although, as we shall see, the Germans saw this possibility in a different light.

It is an old adage in warfare that one man behind fixed defences is worth three attackers. In that respect, fortification was the answer to France's manpower shortage. It was a wise precaution to block off as much of such a long frontier as possible, thus economizing on troops and narrowing the openings available to a potential enemy. There is, however, another side to the coin. The attacker has the advantage in that he can choose the time and place of his attack and, having chosen, can concentrate all his resources at that point. The defender, however, must spread his forces equally at all times; the longer the line, the more men he needs. In theory the perfect defensive position is one that cannot be outflanked, but in the case of the Maginot Line, it could be outflanked both via Belgium and Switzerland. As Clausewitz said, 'Whilst we occupy with our force an unassailable position, we directly refuse the battle, and oblige our enemy to seek for a solution in some other way.'[9] Very true, because no army will assault prepared positions if it can get round them. The French handed the initiative to Germany on a plate by obliging them 'to seek for a solution in some other way'.

One word that was bandied about in the press and by politicians in the 1930s when referring to the Maginot Line was 'impregnable'. Now there is no such thing as an impregnable fortress. Even if constructed in such a position as to be virtually immune from assault, the strongest work must eventually succumb to starvation or lack of water.

In the 55 years that had passed since the Séré de Rivières programme of 1870 the science of fortification had undergone enormous changes. His forts were still individual structures in which the offensive artillery and the defensive infantry were closely grouped together. With the appearance of the high explosive shell, such forts became obvious targets and in many cases steps were taken to remove the guns from the forts and establish them in open batteries in the surrounding country. It was felt that dispersal was the best form of protection, and the forts themselves were covered with heavy layers of concrete. Where guns were still fitted, these were placed in armoured turrets.

In the early 1890s, however, the Germans initiated a radical departure from previous methods when they began construction of the *feste* (fortified group) Kaiser Wilhelm II at Mutzig. This was sited to block the main approach road to Strasbourg through the Vosges. Essentially, the *feste* at Mutzig consisted of two armoured batteries, a number of open batteries and numerous but separate infantry positions, spread over the top of a hill, all connected by underground passages. Thus, the fort, instead of being a monolithic structure, became a piece of defended real estate. This first attempt at splitting the artillery and infantry produced an extremely strong defensive position, completely embedded into the country and presenting a minimal target.

This theme was then extended to Metz and Thionville, where, starting in 1899, the so-called *Mosel Stellung* was constructed. The two fortress towns were surrounded on both sides of the river by a ring of *festes*, each one different, to conform to the available site, but all having the same basic characteristics. Each was surrounded by a barbed-wire obstacle, and in some cases, a ditch, flanked from well-concealed machine-gun positions. Much use was made of camouflage by natural vegetation. The area within was divided into zones isolated from each other by a further obstacle, but connected underground by passages. These zones were either infantry strongpoints or armoured batteries, and each had its own bombproof barracks equipped with life-support systems, such as forced-feed ventilation, power generating plants and water storage tanks. Each *feste* could bring down fire on its neighbours if they were attacked. If one part of such a work succumbed, its remaining garrison could withdraw into another part, sealing off the tunnels and thus prolonging resistance almost indefinitely.[10]

The purpose of the *Mosel Stellung* was to provide the hinge around which the German armies would wheel in the Schlieffen Plan attack through Belgium. By 1914 the forts were almost finished, and although not used during World War I were worked on until 1917. One final refinement in the later ones was the idea of keeping the interior at slight over-pressure, to stop the ingress of poison gas and to expel the fumes from the firing of the guns.

After the experience of Verdun, the French recognized the defects of the forts there. Although not destroyed by bombardment, they lacked underground communication with the rear which meant that reinforcement parties were extremely vulnerable. In the latter part of 1916 they dug tunnels from some of the forts, leading back into dead ground, and built a number of concrete underground barracks. However, they were also aware of the need to extend the defended area of the forts and, even before the war, had begun to experiment with *feste*-type works in the Belfort area.

In 1918 the Metz-Thionville area returned to its former owners and the forts there were avidly studied by French engineers. It is hardly a coincidence that so many structural features of the pre-1914 German works were to be found in the Maginot Line. Even the profile of the concrete parts is remarkably similar. French sources do not acknowledge the affinity, but the *feste* was the obvious ancestor of the Maginot-type fort or *ouvrage*.

A strange paradox is that the old Metz forts enjoyed a brief moment of glory from September to December, 1944, when they were assaulted by an American army corps possessing far greater firepower than the Germans could muster in 1940. Without sighting equipment and garrisoned by troops who had had no training whatsoever in fortress warfare, they withstood bombardment and direct attack, only to succumb finally to lack of food and water. Between the wars they had been ignored by the French who were constructing the Maginot Line further to the north, and only two of them, forts Guentrange and Koenigsmacher at Thionville, were incorporated into the later defences as second-line positions. The latter fort was reduced by the Americans who took three days to winkle out the stubborn defenders section by section, pouring petrol down the ventilators and blowing in the bunkers and tunnel entrances with explosives.[11]

In 1927 the basic programme of the Maginot Line was approved after a number of hearings before the *Conseil Supérieur de la Guerre*, but there was no money immediately available to pay for it. Maginot, out of office, but still president of the Parliamentary Army Commission, managed to persuade that body to permit the sale of certain unused military lands and installations, and Painlevé, at the time War Minister, found some unused funds in the army appropriations. With this they were able to get work started on two experimental sections in February 1928.

The *Commission de Défense des Frontières*, having completed its task, was superseded by the *Commission d'Organisation des Régions Fortifiés* (CORF) which was established by a decree dated 30 September 1927.[12] This body was charged with the practical implementation of the scheme, and was presided over by General Belhague, who was the Inspector-General of engineers. It was the CORF that laid down the basic outline of the works required and activated the design process. The official name for the defences was *Fronts CORF*—hardly very emotive, but at that stage nobody was particularly interested in the subject. A *front CORF* consisted of a number of basic elements, which were shuffled around to comply with the requirements of the terrain to be fortified. Although frequently described by the French as a sytem of defence in depth, it did not cover more than a strip of land up to 12 km back from the frontier.

On crossing the border the enemy would first encounter the *maisons fortes*. These were fortified barracks manned by *gardes mobiles* or armed frontier police, whose job was to impose an initial delay and to pass the alarm back to the main defences. To do this, in addition to their personal weapons, they had equipment for creating road blocks, and were situated at all possible border crossing points.

One or two kilometres to the rear came the first stage of the defences proper—the *avant postes* or advanced posts. These were bunkers, permanently manned and equipped with machine-guns and 47 mm anti-tank guns. At this stage defensive demolitions could be carried out, and the bunkers were protected by obstacles consisting of barbed wire to hinder infantry and sets of rails, embedded in concrete, to stop tanks. Again, their function was to impose a delay; they could also be covered by the fire of the main defences.

The upright rail sections of the standard Maginot Line obstacle system were planted in several rows and at varying heights up to 2 m. Behind them came a barbed-wire entanglement 7 m wide and laid over anti-tank mines. These were round, 30 cm in diameter, and so constructed that they would only detonate when contacted by a weight over 350 kg.

A questionable German source describes two kinds of anti-personnel mine. The first was the spring mine, which was buried in a tube, the mouth of which was covered by a board and some soil. A charge in the base of the tube was detonated by the operation of a trip-wire, which then propelled the mine above ground. At the same time, the flame from the explosion lit a time detonator inside the mine itself, causing it to explode when roughly at head height. The second type was activated by someone stepping on a turf-covered board. This then fell inward, causing the person to stumble forward, and at the same time pulled a wire which exploded a mine in a cavity filled with stones—the twentieth-century version of the *fougasse*.[13]

Behind the *avant postes* and built into the slopes of low hills was the main defensive line, known as the *position de résistance*. This consisted basically of two types of work—the *casemate* and the *ouvrage*. The former term can lead to confusion as it is used in two senses in connection with the Maginot Line. Technically, a casemate is a vaulted structure or chamber designed to house artillery, personnel or stores. The French

28

used it to mean the small blockhouses situated between the main forts, which I will refer to as interval casemates. They also used it in connection with gun chambers in the main forts which fired through embrasures rather than from turrets—casemated batteries.

The main position was again fronted by a continuous obstacle of rails and barbed wire, supplemented in places by an anti-tank ditch. The interval casemates were designed solely to give flanking fire along this obstacle, and had no forward firing artillery. From the front one could only see a bank of earth topped with two or three rusty brown metal domes. These were for observation purposes and in addition were fitted with 50 mm mortars and automatic rifles. Each casemate consisted of two levels—ground floor and basement. The former had one or two firing chambers, depending on whether it had to fire in one or two directions. These had two embrasures covered with armour-plated shields into which were fitted twin Reibell machine-guns. One of the shields was hinged, so that the machine-gun could be swung aside and replaced by a 47 mm anti-tank gun. This was suspended from a rail on the ceiling, and was simply rolled forward and plugged into the open embrasure.

Rails embedded to form an anti-tank obstacle. most of these have since been removed for scrap, but this section can still be seen at La Ferté

Troops manning a 47 mm anti-tank gun in a firing chamber. The twin machine-guns have been swung away to the right and the A/T gun is suspended from a rail on the ceiling. Under the embrasure is a tube for evacuating the spent MG cases into the ditch

The entrance was at the rear, where the concrete was exposed, being fronted by a deep but narrow ditch which was crossed by a removable bridge. This was also flanked by machine-guns and hand-grenade launchers, while the surrounding area could be illuminated by searchlights installed in armoured housings.

The living quarters were situated in the basement, and each unit was self-sufficient for stores and water. There was an electricity generating plant and a mechanical ventilation system which could also be hand operated. Garrisons varied from a dozen to thirty men, commanded by a subaltern. Occasionally the casemates were built as a pair, back to back and connected by a tunnel. This was resorted to where a small hill could be covered by a unit on each side.

The actual forts, spaced, on average, 5 km apart, came in various sizes often depending on the terrain into which they had to be inserted. No two were ever the same, but they all consisted of the same basic elements

TYPICAL INTERVAL CASEMATE

Armament — 3 x twin M.G., 4 automatic rifles, 1 x 47mm A.T., 1 x 50mm mortar.
Ammunition — 120,000 M.G. rounds, 31,000 automatic rifle, 600 A.T. shells,
1,000 mortar bombs plus grenades etc.

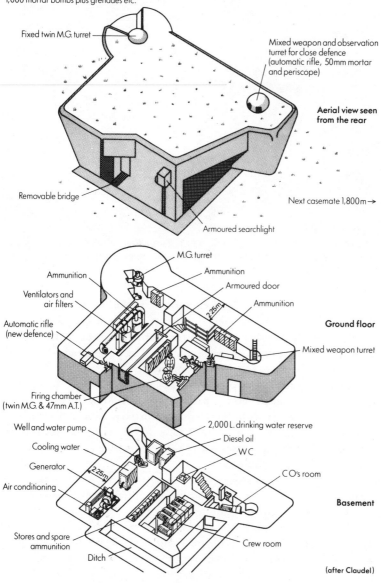

Fixed twin M.G. turret

Mixed weapon and observation
turret for close defence
(automatic rifle, 50mm mortar
and periscope)

**Aerial view seen
from the rear**

Removable bridge

Next casemate 1,800 m →

Armoured searchlight

M.G. turret

Ammunition

Ammunition

Ventilators and
air filters

Armoured door

Ammunition

Automatic rifle
(new defence)

Ground floor

Mixed weapon turret

Firing chamber
(twin M.G. & 47mm A.T.)

Well and water pump

2,000 L. drinking water reserve

Cooling water

Diesel oil

W C

Generator

C O's room

Air conditioning

Basement

Stores and spare
ammunition

Crew room

Ditch

(after Claudel)

31

Ouvrage de Metrich. Personnel entry block flanked by embrasures for machine guns and an anti-tank gun. Note the brackets for supporting the radio antenna and the withdrawable bridge over the ditch

in varying combinations. These elements were the 'blocks', which were the combat units, either artillery or infantry, which projected above the surface, and the entrance blocks at the rear. These were joined by an infrastructure of tunnels and were supported by underground barracks, magazines, generating plant and command posts.

The subterranean parts were located at least 20 m below the surface, and, depending on the terrain, parts of a fort could be anything up to 90 m deep. The entrance blocks could be situated as far as 2–3 km to the rear of the combat area. Construction was carried out mainly by tunnelling, but in some cases where the terrain permitted, the cut and cover method was employed.

Generally, the service area was well to the rear, not far from the entrances. In the larger forts, the latter were of two types, personnel and stores, and were built into the reverse slopes of the ridge of hills on which the main defences were situated. A 60 cm gauge railway ran into the stores entry through a wide steel grid door. Both types of entrance were self-defensible, with observation domes on top and flanking chambers to cover the doorways and the ditch, armed with machine-

General view of the stores entry block at Metrich. Such blocks normally had two mixed-weapon turrets on top and the embrasures were fitted for twin machine-guns or a 47 mm anti-tank gun

guns and anti-tank weapons. As far as the entrances the external narrow-gauge railway used diesel locomotives, bringing up supplies from the main depots to the rear.

Immediately inside the stores entry was an armoured air-tight door, in front of which was a deep pit crossed by a removeable bridge as an anti-tank precaution. This in turn was fronted by another armoured door covered by the embrasures of an interior firing chamber. Only when all those barriers had been surmounted could the enemy penetrate the main gallery. Normally this ran forward at the same level as the entry block, but in some cases lay deeper. Some forts had a gentle slope running down from the entrance, while others used a lift to reach the main gallery floor.

Proceeding forward along the main gallery, which could be anything up to 7 m wide and 6 m high, one came to the main magazine complex. This consisted of a number of chambers arranged on a grid pattern, each part of which was closed off by a fire door. The ammunition was stored, ready for use, in square metal cages (*chassis*) which were transported forward to the blocks by the internal railway network. This was powered

The main railway shunting area of a large *ouvrage* (Hackenberg) looking forward along the main tunnel. The entrance to the left leads to the main magazine (M1). In the background where the tunnel narrows, it can be closed off by a 17-ton blast door

The operating theatre in the sick bay at Hackenberg (Kristensen)

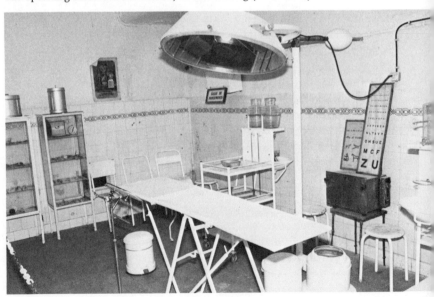

by current supplied by overhead cables, and the trucks and locomotives were parked in a shunting area near the magazine. The whole magazine area could be isolated from the rest of the fort by a 17-ton door which closed automatically in case of an explosion.

Situated near the personnel entrance was the main barracks complex. The sleeping accommodation consisted of three-tier iron beds reaching almost up to the celings of the plain vaulted chambers. Those on the top level had hardly any headroom. In the same area were the dining rooms, canteen, kitchens, hospital etc. The latter was equipped to perform operations, although, where possible, casualties were evacuated to the rear depots. One hoary old legend concerns the disposal of the dead from Maginot Line forts. The story has it that they were to be reduced in acid and washed out down the drains; another version refers to vast beds of quicklime where corpses could be buried. The reality was less macabre. Each fort had a number of coffins made of galvanized metal and a properly fitted mortuary. Anyway, large numbers of casualties were not envisaged.

Next to the barracks came the *usine*, which was the power station of the fort. This was equipped with a number of diesel generators which

Transformer and power distribution plant in the *usine* of a large *ouvrage* (Kristensen)

were fed from large fuel storage tanks. Normally these were not used, as the forts were supplied with current from the French national grid. The power lines entered the ground well to the rear and were deeply buried. In the case of the line to one fort being disrupted, it could be supplied from its neighbours via a link line; only in the case of total failure would the internal services be called upon. The *usine* also housed the transformer equipment which supplied current, direct or alternating, at the voltages required for different purposes. The normal tension was 440 volts alternating, but the railway ran on 600 volts direct, for example. Another part of the complex housed the filter system. Fresh air was pumped in from the rear and, in case of gas attack, passed through banks of filters before being supplied to the blocks under pressure. Used air was expelled through the turrets, and the ventilation system also coped with the foul air from the toilets, kitchens, used cartridge stores, etc.

Drainage caused some problems for the designers. Where possible, a natural slope was used to dispose of effluent outside the forts, and in some cases these drains could be used as emergency exits. To stop anybody getting in, they were so equipped that a machine-gun could fire down them. One problem was that the soldiers used the toilets to dispose of old socks, razor blades and empty bottles, which led to blockages.[14]

The garrisons numbered from around 200 to 1,200 in the largest forts. The French used the word *equipage* or crew, and to carry the navy simile further, they were organized into watches—duty, stand-by and rest. (After the Line had been manned for the first time in 1936, at the time of the Rhineland crisis, groups of men were sent to the navy to study the organization on board warships.) The fortress commander was either a major or a lieutenant-colonel. The men themselves, mostly technical specialists, were chosen from among the younger soldiers, contrary to past practice whereby fortress duty was reserved for the elderly and infirm.

All those who have written about the Maginot Line from personal experience testify to a remarkable *esprit de corps* among the troops who served there, and there is no evidence of the moral collapse suffered by so many French units in 1940.

There were three types of soldier serving on garrison duty in the Line: the infantry, whose job was to guard the entrances, man the internal defensive positions and to crew the infantry combat blocks for surface defence; the artillery, who manned the larger guns, provided the fire control system and organized the ammunition services; and the engineers, who were divided into several groups. Of these, the electro-mechanics were responsible for the machinery in the *usine*, the railway engineers for the internal transport network, and the telegraphists for the signals equipment. Finally, there were general engineers, responsible for running repairs to the structures and, harking back to old-fashioned fortress warfare, for counter-mining. Some of the forts had listening galleries running out into the open country in front of them. There, men were posted to listen for attempts to tunnel into the fort, and to prepare charges to eliminate enemy mines. Things had not changed much since the days of Vauban.

The armament was divided into infantry and artillery weapons—close-in and distant defence. The actual number of guns mounted was the minimum required to defend the position and would be supple-mented in wartime by the artillery of the interval troops, which will be discussed later. It will be recalled that, prior to 1916, the guns of the old forts at Verdun and other places had been removed for use in the field; the designers of the Maginot Line made certain that this would not happen again. They used guns that only fitted fortress mountings, although the ammunition was the same as for a field piece of comparable calibre.[15]

The infantry were equipped with the following weapons:

50 mm mortar, installed either in a turret or a casemate

47 mm anti-tank gun, model 1934

37 mm anti-tank gun, model 1934

25 mm anti-tank gun, either long or shortened, introduced at the beginning of 1935

Twin Reibell MAC 1931 F machine-gun, which was the main anti-personnel weapon

Automatic rifles, in the observation turrets and for internal defence

Grenade launchers

The artillery blocks were armed with the following:

Various models of the 75 mm gun, fitted either in pairs in turrets or singly in casemates—range 1,200 m

75 mm shortened model of 1932—maximum range 9,500 m

81 mm mortar—range 3,500 m

135 mm howitzer—range 5,600 m

The total number of guns mounted in the defences of the north-east and the Alpine frontier was only 344, which is surprisingly few considering the length of the front.

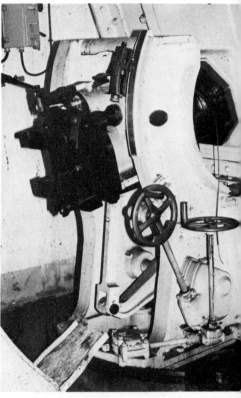

81 mm mortar (casemate version) capable of some 15 rounds per minute. This weapon, now in a museum, traversed on a fixed bed

135 mm howitzer emplaced in a casemate. The wheels on the right are for elevating and traversing the weapon, and behind is the chute for disposing of empty cartridge cases (Kristensen)

This armament was installed in the various combat blocks grouped around the command post, which was reached by sub-tunnels branching off from the main gallery. The command post was the 'brain' or nerve centre of each fort where all the various communication systems came together. From there the fire of the artillery was controlled and the defence of the fort co-ordinated.

The blocks were the 'sharp' ends of the forts, and the only parts on the surface, although their lowest parts were at the same level as the main gallery system. There, each block had its own magazine, supplied by railway, its crew quarters and command post. The ammunition containers were transferred from the trucks of the train and hung from

Entrance block of a small *ouvrage* (Bois du Four). The small grilles cover the exhaust pipes from the generating plant

overhead rails. From there they could easily be moved into the lifts leading to the loading positions. Beside each lift was a personnel staircase which twisted round the chute that was used to dispose of the empty cartridge cases.

The actual blocks were built of reinforced concrete, and in front, towards the enemy, they were banked with earth. Only at the rear was the concrete exposed. When the test came in 1940, this proved to be a weakness. The rear walls had been left comparatively thin (1.5 m) on purpose so that if the enemy succeeded in occupying a block, the walls could be easily broken down. The problem was that, by outflanking the Line, it was the enemy that arrived at the rear of the blocks, and the thin concrete proved to be no match for the 88 mm flak guns that were used as battering weapons.

The roofs were much thicker, being designed in most cases to withstand bombardment by such guns as the World War I German 420 mm howitzer and by 1-ton aerial bombs. The basic theme was to build the blocks according to the weapons likely to be used against them. The various types of observation dome were all that protruded from the roof as a fixture. The artillery turrets when retracted were

above   Cloche GFM (mixed-weapon turret) on top of an interval casemate in the Montmédy bridgehead. Thickness of steel, 25 cm. This has the ball-joint type embrasure for the automatic rifle. The metal loops in the foreground were for attaching camouflage nets

right   Observation turret at Soetrich. The cover on top closed off the periscope aperture. Note the application of an adhesive camouflage substance

below   Close-up of a twin 135 mm howitzer turret in the raised position. Block 11 at Metrich

virtually invisible. Much use was made of camouflage, with built-in fastenings for nets, and in some cases, the observation domes were coated with pieces of natural stone. In addition, dummy turrets were installed, made up from ordinary metal.

The actual artillery blocks were classified into casemate blocks and turret blocks, depending on how the armament was mounted. This description of the basic elements of the main line of defence is naturally a generalization, as no two forts were ever the same, and the basic units were juggled about to conform with the terrain.

During the period 1939–40 a further line of entrenchments and pill-boxes was constructed to the rear of the main position, behind the entrance blocks. Also to the rear were a number of barracks which housed the regular garrisons in peacetime, under less onerous conditions than those prevailing inside the forts. The whole defended zone was dotted with large numbers of shelters and observation posts for the interval troops. The latter were intended to solve the problem of the immobility of the defences, their mission being to react flexibly to an attack. They were drawn from normal army units and were equipped with the usual field weapons including the only anti-aircraft guns deployed in the Maginot Line. They also had the only artillery capable of shelling positions over the German border. The fortress artillery lacked this capability, which was one of the valid criticisms levelled at the Line. The reason for this lay partly in the defensive philosophy behind the construction, but the inability to deter concentrations of troops massing for an attack imposed a serious disadvantage.

The main reason, however, was a purely technical one. The Maginot-type turrets were retractable, being raised into the firing position by heavy counter-weights. Lowered, they presented only mushroom shaped domes from which projectiles would be deflected. This meant that only guns with extremely short barrels could be fitted into turrets which were restricted to a diameter of 4 m; projecting barrels would have necessitated slots in the surrounding armour plate apron. A grand total of 152 such retractable turrets were fitted into the Maginot Line. The steel was generally 30 cm thick, and the weight of one for a pair of 75 mm guns was no less than 280 tons.

Thus, to sum up, the *fronts CORF*, or Maginot Line sections, consisted of a number of defensive positions stretching back, on average, 12 km from the frontier. The initial lines were designed to delay the enemy, to give time for the main line to be manned (half an hour in the case of a surprise attack). The main line consisted of interval casemates spread out between forts of various sizes, fronted by a continuous anti-tank and personnel obstacle. In the rear was a final line of defence constructed after the war had begun. To support the fortifications there were the interval troops, who formed the mobile corps of resistance.

DIAGRAM TO ILLUSTRATE STORAGE AND SUPPLY OF AMMUNITION IN A LARGE OUVRAGE

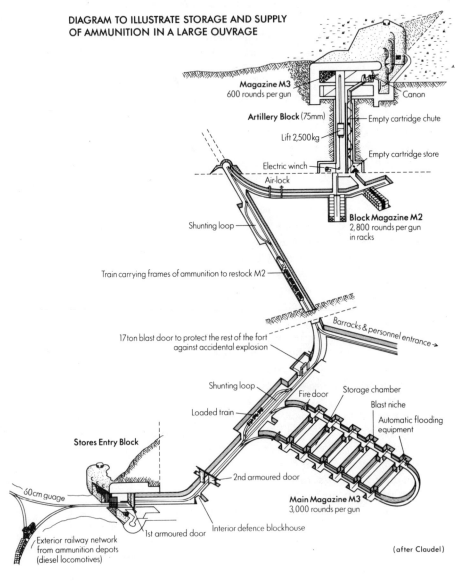

Magazine M3
600 rounds per gun

Canon

Artillery Block (75mm)

Empty cartridge chute

Lift 2,500 kg

Empty cartridge store

Electric winch

Air-lock

Block Magazine M2
2,800 rounds per gun
in racks

Shunting loop

Train carrying frames of ammunition to restock M2

Barracks & personnel entrance →

17 ton blast door to protect the rest of the fort
against accidental explosion

Shunting loop

Fire door

Storage chamber

Blast niche

Loaded train

Automatic flooding
equipment

Stores Entry Block

60 cm guage

2nd armoured door

Main Magazine M3
3,000 rounds per gun

Exterior railway network
from ammunition depots
(diesel locomotives)

1st armoured door

Interior defence blockhouse

(after Claudel)

Chapter 4

Finance and progress of construction

The CORF, formed in September 1927, was essentially a co-ordinating body made up of representatives of various arms, such as engineers and artillery, and it operated from regional delegations at Metz and Strasbourg. The actual work was carried out by civilian contractors, supervised by engineer departments specially set up for the purpose. These were strategically located at such places as Nice, Bitche, Thionville etc. By January 1936, the bulk of the initial programme had been completed, and the CORF set-up was dissolved.

The locations of the actual works constructed differed from those proposed by the Frontier Defence Commission in that the Upper Alsace Fortified Region was eliminated. Instead, the whole of the Rhine frontier from Basle in the south to Fort Louis in the north was defended by a double line of infantry casemates. One line ran more or less along the banks of the river, and the other, some three or four kilometres to the rear, followed the north/south road from Lauterbourg through Strasbourg to Neuf Brisach and Basle. These works had no integral artillery, as it was felt that the river itself was a sufficiently imposing barrier. However, it was assumed that interval troops with adequate artillery would be available to cover all possible crossing sites.

In addition to the Rhine defences there were the two fortified regions in the north-east, as originally proposed. On the left was the Metz RF (*Région Fortifiée*) which ran originally from the Moselle to the north of Thionville, to Téting on the River Nied. This was almost immediately extended westwards as far as Longuyon, to cover the Briey industrial area.

A typical interval casemate of the type built along the Rhine front, situated near Neuf Brisach. On the left, the main embrasures fitted for machine and anti-tank guns, could only fire along the flank

Cloche GFM on top of a Rhine casemate, looking towards the river. This turret has the more common *crenau* type embrasure into which an automatic rifle, a 50 mm mortar or an episcope could be fitted

On the right was the Lauter RF which ran between Bitche and the Rhine. These two regions were known as the *anciens fronts* and represent the classic period of CORF-type construction—the Maginot Line proper.

There was, however, other work carried out by the CORF in the south which has never been reckoned as part of what became popularly known as the Maginot Line. The defences in the Alps were prompted by the rise of Mussolini, which posed a threat to French security in the area. A series of short separate fronts were constructed to block the main passes leading into Italy—the Petit St Bernard, Mont Cenis, Col de Fréjus, Montgenèvre, Larche and Restefond. To the south there was a continuous line running from Mont Mounier to the sea at Menton—the Alpes Maritimes RF.

The final place to be fortified by the CORF was Corsica, which was regarded as an unsinkable aircraft carrier, neatly situated between France and her North African colonies. The likely enemy landing places on the island were defended by infantry casemates, around Bastia, St Florent and the southern tip.

As far back as February 1927, Paul Painlevé, who was then War Minister, authorized three of the planned twenty sections to be put out to tender. These first steps were financed from the sale of surplus military lands and excess budget monies, as had been proposed by André Maginot. Although the two men were political opponents, both were dedicated to seeing the fortifications completed, and thus managed to bury their differences. This early work, which was of an experimental nature, was used to test the practicability of the various design studies.

It was on replacing Painlevé as War Minister in 1929 that Maginot was able to play a decisive but brief role in the history of the fortifications named after him. He himself admitted that he was only carrying on where his predecessor had left off, and in 1935, Édouard Herriot proposed that the works should be called the Painlevé Line. One could argue that the latter did more to ensure the completion of the fortifications than Maginot did. With Maginot in charge, however, a new sense of urgency was imparted to the proceedings on account of the imminent withdrawal from the Rhineland, six years earlier than had been laid down at the Treaty of Versailles. Although the area would still be demilitarized and Hitler was but a small cloud looming on the horizon, it was felt that France would lose her protective security zone. Thus construction of the defences was an immediate necessity. The problem was how to pay for them. The Chamber of Deputies was not renowned for generosity in respect of military expenditure, especially when the majority were convinced that no threat existed. It was difficult to persuade politicians to vote money for defence when solemn treaties proclaimed the outlawry of war.

By 1929 the whole subject of fortifications for the frontiers had become public property, and was being discussed, generally negatively, in the press. Weimar Germany was not considered a danger, and the socialists and communists were preaching universal disarmament.

The original estimate, made in 1928, had been 3,760 million francs (more or less impossible to render in present day currency). Paradoxically, this was destined to be successively reduced, at the same time as the scope of the works was being increased, *and* with rampant inflation in the background. The initial proposal submitted to Parliament was for 3,140 millions (in December 1929) when the 1930 budget was being debated.[16] More or less single-handed, Maginot lobbied members, selling patriotism to the right wing and the creation of employment to the left. On 10 December he made a major speech in the Chamber in which he said,

We could scarcely dream of building a form of Great Wall of France which would anyway be far too costly. Instead, we have foreseen powerful but flexible means of organizing defence, based on the principles of taking advantage of the terrain, and of establishing a continuous line of fire everywhere.

His tactics were based on deliberate understatement, backed by the realities of the loss of the Rhineland and the fact that recruitment would reach crisis point by 1935. He also naturally emphasized the defensive nature of the fortifications. When the matter came up again on 28 December, the Chamber, possibly sleepy after the Christmas festivities, voted the sum of 2,900 million francs, to be spread over a period of four years, without the need for annual review.

Maginot's contribution to the history of the French frontier defences was that he conjured up the money to pay for them. However, the sum represented a reduction of 860 millions from the original estimate, money that would have been vital for realizing the original programme in its entirety. An incomplete fortification is just as bad as none at all, and in the end, further sums had to be obtained. The final figure is impossible to give accurately, but was probably around 6,000 million francs in the currency of 1940, roughly double the original figure estimated.

left Observation post at the Cap Martin *ouvrage* (Alpes Maritimes RF). This was the work nearest to the Mediterranean which overlooked Menton and guarded the coast road along the Riviera

below Casemate artillery block in the Alpes Maritimes RF (Sainte Agnes). The shape of the concrete is slightly different from that of similar blocks in the north-east regions. Two embrasures for 135 mm howitzers and two for 75 mm guns

Officers' married quarters at one of the rear barracks designed for occupation during peacetime

Thus the scope of the work had to be tailored to fit the available funds, at a time when the value of the franc was diminishing. And, as work progressed, the inevitable modifications were required, which also had to be paid for from the original appropriations. This led to a watering down of the proposals and the omission of many features that were considered necessary.

Work got underway at the end of 1929 on the large *ouvrages* of Rochonvillers, Hackenberg, Simserhof and Hochwald, these being the key points of the Metz and Lauter RF respectively. In 1930 the rest of the work on the *anciens fronts* was started, with the excavation of tunnels and ditches, and on the concrete for the interior and the blocks. The phase was completed between 1932 and 1933, when fitting-out was started—the various types of ordnance and their associated armour protection, the mechanical equipment and the interior fixtures. As in the case of the ground work, trials were conducted at the large forts, the results of which were studied before being passed for series production.

Already, by August 1930, the reductions previously mentioned had become apparent. This resulted in cutting down the number of blocks originally foreseen for some forts, increasing the distance between interval casemates, and in an extreme case, replacing two small forts by casemates. Other forts never received their entrance blocks.

By 1935 the first generation works were more or less complete, although detail work was still in progress. They were fully garrisoned

An interval casemate in the Montmédy bridgehead, converted for agricultural purposes, seen from the rear

for the first time in March 1936, on the occasion of Germany's re-militarization of the Rhineland. Hitler's gigantic bluff worked, and the only French reaction was to occupy the Maginot Line. Hitler himself admitted that his few troops would have fled if one shot had been fired at them.

The manning of the Line, however, was opportune, in that it highlighted a large number of defects, such as dampness. As soon as the crisis was over, the garrisons were stood down and the engineers returned to make a large number of modifications, including an extensive drying out.[17]

In the meanwhile the political framework under which the original scheme had been envisaged had changed, for the worse as far as France was concerned. The Saar region, which made a gap between the two fortified regions, had been left unfortified under the assumption that the area would, after the plebiscite in 1935, either go to France or would remain under the control of the League of Nations, in which case the defences could be based on the River Saar. In the plebiscite, however, the population voted to be united with Germany. This meant that the area between Bitche and the Saar, the Rohrbach plateau, was vulnerable to invasion. As a result the Lauter RF was extended as far as Wittring on the Saar, as the first of what were known as the *nouvelles fronts*, built between 1934 and 1938. Although the architecture of this second generation of works was somewhat more sophisticated than the earlier

49

ones, the lack of resources led to the almost total exclusion of turreted artillery.

The other new fronts were a direct result of Belgium's declaration of permanent neutrality in 1936, which forced the French to defend their frontier with Belgium when it was far too late and the money almost exhausted.

The immediate reaction was the decision to create *l'ossature permanente d'un champ de bataille*, the permanent framework for a battlefield, consisting of field works, barbed wire and pill-boxes.[18] The General Staff were still convinced that the only way to defend the northern frontier was to advance into Belgium, and in this they were supported by Britain, who would not tolerate hostile occupation of the Channel ports. Besides, the army was under increasing pressure from the politicians of the frontier departments to build defences. Even if the funds had been available, the Maginot Line could not have been extended for the reasons already stated. Painfully slowly a line of small bunkers was constructed between Dunkirk and the Line proper at Longuyon. The exact number has never been counted, but it ran into

Rear entrance to an interval casemate, reached by a retractable bridge over the ditch. Note wire rail along roof for fixing camouflage netting. This view gives an indication of the thickness of the covering concrete

several thousand, built under the auspices of the local military commanders. Many of them were still unfinished in 1940, lacking such vital parts as metal embrasure shields.

Inserted into this new line of primitive defences were the final examples of CORF work to be undertaken. The fortified sectors of Montmédy and Maubeuge were constructed as *nouvelles fronts*, consisting only of infantry blocks and casemates, and a few small works were undertaken in front of Valenciennes.

The remaining gap between the two fortified regions was designated the zone of inundations. Between Téting and the Saar, centred on Puttelange, a number of dams were constructed which would be opened when there was an alert. In theory, this would produce an impassable water barrier, which would be backed up by a line of interval casemates with interlocking fields of fire, supported on either flank by powerful artillery forts. Construction of the casemates started as late as 1938, and they too were unfinished in 1940, while the flanking forts ended as small infantry works.

Although its mission was not fully completed, the CORF was abolished at the end of December 1935. From then on, responsibility for the fortifications was vested in the military regions, a decision that had adverse consequences. The global authority of the CORF, which had ensured a continuity of design and construction, was lost, to the detriment of the overall concept.

By March 1936, when they were first occupied, the main defences in the north-east were completed and armed, although the many defects that became apparent were still being slowly rectified in 1940. As a result of adverse political conditions a number of less sophisticated extensions were built which were almost totally lacking in integral artillery. Finally, the defences which extended towards the English Channel were no more than simple bunkers and field works.

Chapter 5

The Czech 'Maginot Line'

Prior to 1914 French strategy had been based on the so-called Triple Entente—the alliance with Britain and Russia—designed to force Germany to fight a war on two fronts. In 1918, after the elimination of Russia as a credible diplomatic entity, France had to re-think her foreign policy. She turned then to the number of small states that had been created in Eastern Europe from the wreckage of the Austro-Hungarian Empire. This became known as the Little Entente, which in reality was a group of treaties combining Czechoslovakia, Romania and Yugoslavia, with all of whom France was allied. The grouping was completed by a treaty with Poland. The problem was that such allies were no substitute for Russia. They lacked her material resources and could not agree among themselves. It also caused some estrangement with the traditional ally, Britain, who became suspicious of French ambitions in Eastern Europe. However, France never profited from the Entente and totally failed to come to the help of her allies in their hour of need. To do so she would have required an army capable of going beyond her borders.

The only connection that French eastern policy has with the subject of this book is that France exported her belief in the value of fixed defences. Poland was not impressed, but in Czechoslovakia a mini Maginot Line was built during the early 1930s under the supervision of French engineer officers. Although not as sophisticated as the works in north-eastern France, it did feature a few deep forts with turreted artillery.

Like its French counterpart, however, it only covered part of the main frontier with Germany. It ran from Ostrava in the east, where the German, Czech and Polish borders met, to Nachod, a distance of some 175 km. It thus protected the eastern part of the frontier with German

Silesia and stopped just where the Riesengebirge mountains started, although the latter had not proved to be a barrier to armies in the past. From there, light defences covered the rest of the border where Czechoslovakia projected into German and Austrian territory. There was, however, a wide gap apparently devoid of defences where the Bohemian forest runs over into Bavaria, opposite Regensburg. Prague was also ringed by the same light defences, of the barbed-wire and pill-box variety.

The only details available of the Czech fortifications are in a wartime German publication which states that there were no retractable artillery turrets, which meant that the muzzles of the guns were exposed, and that the forts had far fewer blocks than comparable French ones. This is hardly surprising when one considers the drain on the resources of a large country such as France that was imposed by the fortification programme.[19]

One Czech source states that the anti-tank obstacles were not as strong as the upright rails used in France. However, the main difference seems to be that the artillery, such as it was, was installed on the reverse slopes of hills, rather than on the forward slopes as in the Maginot Line. This had the advantage of making the turrets invisible to ground observation, but tests carried out by the Germans after they had occupied the defences proved that the embrasures could easily have been blocked by debris rolling down on to them.[20]

In the outcome the expense proved to have been pointless. With the connivance of France and Britain, Czechoslovakia was forced to hand over the border territories to Germany in 1938, who thus obtained the fortifications free of charge. Their real usefulness, however, had already been weakened. Through the *Anschluss* with Austria, Germany had gained possession of the lightly defended southern border.

Once they had occupied the Czech works, German experts descended on them by the score. A whole series of artillery tests were carried out, and the unit that had been earmarked to land in their rear in the case of resistance to the takeover, the 7th *Flieger* division, carried out the attack as a practice run. The main windfall, however, was a propaganda one. A number of troops were photographed inside the fortifications, which were then issued to the press as pictures of deep forts inside the Siegfried Line, which had none. As these photographs were first published in 1939, they cannot have been taken elsewhere.[21]

Initially, however, the Germans had assumed that they would have to fight for Czechoslovakia. The first thoughts on the matter were laid down in a document dated 24 June 1937, initiated by Field-Marshal von Blomberg. This was based on the premise either of war in the west as a result of a surprise attack by France, or of war in the south-east. The latter eventuality was given the codename *Fall Grün*—Case Green. The *Anschluss* with Austria cleared the way to a certain extent for the final reckoning with the unfortunate Czechs, but although the main defences had been outflanked, they still represented a deterrent to the Germans. On 17 May 1938, Hitler, from Berchtesgarten, asked OKW in Berlin for precise information about the Czech fortifications, and Lt-Colonel Zeitzler replied in a lengthy 'most secret' telegram, making it clear that they were likely to cause problems.

The whole sordid aspect of the negotiations leading up to the Munich agreement do not concern us here. Sold out by their allies, the Czechs collapsed, giving Hitler all that he wanted without the necessity of fighting. His military advisers seem to have been relieved, as Keitel testified during his trial at Nuremberg:

We were extraordinarily happy that it had not come to a military operation because ... we had always been of the opinion that our means of attack against the frontier fortifications in Czechoslovakia were insufficient. From a purely military point of view we lacked the means for an attack which involved the piercing of the frontier fortifications.

Manstein, who was probably the most accomplished German commander agreed with the above judgement. Also at Nuremberg, he stated, 'If a war had broken out ... had Czechoslovakia defended herself, we would have been held up by her fortifications, for we did not have the means to break through.'

At the time Hitler had not been convinced by the objections of his generals, but he said later, 'When after Munich we were in a position to examine Czechoslovak military strength from within, what we saw of it greatly disturbed us; we had run a serious danger.'

It seems clear that the knowledge gained from examining the Czech works strengthened German determination not to attack the Maginot Line, but rather to seek 'a solution elsewhere'.[22]

Chapter 6

The Myth

One inescapable fact about building fortifications is that they cannot be hidden. Vast excavations have to be made and quantities of soil disposed of. Large numbers of workmen are required, not all of whom can be screened, and in the twentieth century the advent of the aeroplane has meant that any large scale construction work is almost impossible to conceal. As the Maginot Line was built within a few kilometres of the German border much of the work would have been visible from the air without even infringing French air space. In addition, short of declaring the whole area to be a military zone and entirely evacuating the civilian population, which would have meant vast sums in compensation and much discussion in the press, the secret could never have been kept.

During the construction period there were frequent spy scares, which was hardly surprising in view of the fact that the area in which the defences were situated was one of divided loyalties. Alsace-Lorraine had a definite pro-German minority, and there were always harmless tourists who were at liberty to cross the border. Many of the contractors were local firms, and it would have been easy for the German intelligence service to infiltrate agents on to their payrolls.

On the other hand any fortification scheme is a form of deterrent and a deterrent that is secret is useless. You have to present your potential enemy with knowledge of your power, preferably exaggerated, in order to deter him from attacking you. Therefore you 'allow' him insight into the scope of your military hardware. As the purpose of the Maginot Line was to deter Germany from making a surprise attack, no attempt was made to keep the fortifications such a secret. However, their detail arrangements were subject to strict security.

All the Parliamentary debates on the subject were available for public scrutiny, and thus became of interest to the international press. The French newspapers of the period were violently partisan and, in view of the controversy surrounding the decision to build fortifications and the general pacifist atmosphere at the time, successive governments were attacked for profligacy. The reaction, naturally, was to justify the expense and to inflate the value of the defences, both for internal and external consumption. However, the more justification that was needed, the more the 'leaks' drifted into hyperbole, which in turn inspired the Maginot myth. Looking at newspaper accounts of the 1930s with the sober eye of today, one cannot but be amazed that such nonsense was believed. Vivien Rowe, in his book *The Great Wall of France,* gives a fairly full summary of the utterances of the British press in this respect.

German apologists later speciously claimed that the building of the Maginot Line amid a blaze of publicity was intended to force them to violate Belgian neutrality, and thus negatively influence world opinion. However, having done so once before, they would probably have done it again anyway. Britain, with her power to impose blockade, was just as great an enemy as France, and any German staff officer worth his salary would have been aware that Britain would always intervene to help France, if only to keep another European power away from the Channel ports. What is often forgotten is the fact that when the Maginot Line in the north-east was conceived, the panzer division had not been invented—armoured warfare was only wishful thinking on the part of a handful of junior officers. If the French were imagining warfare in 1918 terms, so were the other European general staffs. A theory has been advanced which suggests that the Belgian frontier was purposely left weak so as to force the intervention of Britain in the event of an invasion; the French were well aware that there was much sympathy in Britain for the plight of Germany. There is, however, no documentary evidence for this, and the decision was based on sound reasons. There may have been some discussion of the idea in the background, and the General Staff may have been aware of it as a possible side effect.

As early as 18 May 1928 the fortifications attracted the notice of the British press, before there had been much public discussion of the matter in France itself. The *Daily News* wrote, 'A wall of concrete and steel built into the ground, heavily fortified and stretching from the North Sea to the Mediterranean, is expected to be built as part of France's preparation for national defence.' One does not know whether this story was obtained by an eager correspondent or 'leaked', but at the time there was no thought at all of building anything on such a scale. The article, however, was a pointer of things to come. Newspapers print what their readers want to hear, and the real facts could easily have been obtained by an astute journalist. With few exceptions, the press did little to promote the truth and put the scheme in its right perspective.

The next spate of publicity came in 1930, after Maginot had secured the necessary finance, an event which had received wide coverage in the French press. In October of that year he paid a visit to the works then in progress in the north-east, and on his return wrote a letter to General Belhague which was subsequently published. In it he expressed his satisfaction with what he had seen and, probably with an eye to German readers, he added his conclusion that the work would be finished by 1934, which was a blatant exaggeration. As far as the extent of the fortifications was concerned, Maginot never made any grandiose claims in his public utterances. In a memorandum to the League of Nations on the eve of the disarmament conference in January 1932, he laid great emphasis on the defensive purpose of the works in the north-east. It is perhaps unfortunate that this was to be virtually his last official pronouncement, as he died on 7 January, after a short illness. Had he lived, he might well have lent the strength of his personality to toning down the official euphoria with which the fortifications were treated, as well as shaking France out of the resulting complacency. Way back in 1922, General Guillaumat had said, 'It is dangerous to let the false and demoralizing notion spread that once we have fortifications the inviolability of our country is assured, and that they are a substitute for the labour of preparing wills, hearts and minds.'

A reasonably accurate view of the scope of the Maginot Line was printed in the *Daily Mail* on 22 October 1930, obtained from a French reporter who had been allowed to visit the sites. The first of the really fanciful reports was in July 1931, when it was stated that the extra credits obtained from the Chamber were 'to complete the great ring of fortifications along the Belgian, German and Italian frontiers, as part of the great Foch scheme of national defence'. It is difficult to see where Foch came in, as his idea had been for an immediate dash across the Rhine. Whoever dreamed up such a concoction of half-truths must have had a strong imagination or been the victim of an officially inspired falsehood.

The first of the really big stories appeared in the *Daily Express* on 16 May 1933, on the occasion of an outbreak of spy mania in Alsace—they had Brown Shirts under the bed in those days. With all the authority of a leading newspaper, the article stated, 'The French have spent officially £190,000,000 completing a chain of underground forts from the English Channel to the Vosges, in which whole army corps can live underground fully provisioned for a year'.

Such arrant nonsense was but a foretaste of revelations to come. A reporter must have been despatched at once and the following day he cabled thus:

I embarked today on a perilous pilgrimage to the battlefields of the next war ... No man had yet succeeded in locating the exact position of the mystery defences, in gauging their strength, appearance and cost. 'Go at your own peril', a high official of the War Ministry said to me when I informed him of my intention ... Along the scattered line of defences north of Metz, behind Belgium where moveable forts, strange modern devices with rolls of barbed wire, armaments and guns, travel from place to place, wherever they are needed, like lumbering tanks, my way lies.

The correspondent must have covered an awful lot of ground in one day—if he went anywhere at all. The frontiers were not closed and there would have been nothing to stop him wandering about at will, as long as he had not tried to enter any actual building site.

The story continued the next day, under the name of Pembroke Stephens:

Nothing to show for all the millions of pounds, the years of work. The forts are invisible to the passers-by, they are invisible from the air as well. Not even an air photograph can betray the exact position of the French forts.

The final twist came a few days later, on 24 May, again from the pen of Mr Stephens:

Beginning my journey at Dunkirk, on the English Channel, touching Belgium, Luxembourg and the Saar, down the Rhine and the Italian Alps, and along the Mediterranean coast to Toulon, the chief military, naval and air port of France, a week on the road, and rarely out of sight of a French fort.

Fortunately, owing to the ephemeral nature of the material, public memories of newspaper articles are short-lived. A correspondent who is rarely out of sight of forts that he had described a few days before as being invisible does tend to stretch credulity to the limit. It is true that the French frontiers are littered with forts, but most of them are eighteenth and nineteenth-century works. At the time of writing, he would have seen little evidence of anything, except in the north-east and along the Rhine.

Not only the *Daily Express* was guilty of blatant misinformation. Most of the newspapers printed stories in a similar vein. Even the *Daily Telegraph* got into the act by stating on 30 April 1933, 'The French fortifications will, when finished, stretch from the English Channel to the Mediterranean'. All this was to disregard totally the public controversy in France itself and the frequent debates in the Chamber, upon such questions as to whether or not the money could be found to extend the works. Besides, any competent journalist could have travelled along the Belgian frontier and would not have seen a single spade in action on a military project at that time.

However, by 1932 Hitler had arrived on the scene and had torn up the military clauses of the Treaty of Versailles. It was thus in French interests to inflate the value of their deterrent. It is probable that the journalistic efforts were a mixture of wishful thinking on the part of official informants and the need for a gripping story. After all, the reality of the Maginot Line was somewhat prosaic

In September 1934, the prestigious *Revue des Deux Mondes* printed an article entitled *Nos Fortifications du Nord-Est*, by General Debeney, ex-chief of staff of the French army and member of the *Commission de défense du territoire*. He knew what he was talking about, and apart from his flowery prose, he produced an excellent factual account of the whole concept of the defensive scheme. He included a timetable of the various stages since the birth of the idea and went through the whole of the strategic controversy. He stated exactly what areas were to be fortified, and why. Naturally he gave no specific details of construction, but made a number of valid criticisms, including the short range of the guns and the need for air observation.

The important point is that, as early as 1934, an authoritative and concise exploration of the subject was available to anyone who could read. In the same year Pétain, as War Minister, made the already quoted statement of the necessity to advance into Belgium. To appease the politicians from the northern areas, credits were voted for fortifications, but only the trifling sum of 292 million francs was left to pay for the defence from Montmédy to the sea (by then, the main part of the Maginot Line had already swallowed up some 5,000 millions). Pétain's predecessor put the matter in perspective when he said, 'We came to the conclusion that for reasons perhaps more psychological than military, it was essential to vote credits for fortifying the northern areas.' This decision was seized upon by the press to mean the extension of the Maginot Line and, according to Alistair Horne, 'the government wholeheartedly encouraged it in this act of self-deception'.[23]

Erroneous press reports continued to appear thoughout 1935 and 1936, becoming more frequent during the Rhineland crisis. During the summer of 1935 the name Maginot Line appeared for the first time, and in September an English newspaper (*The Evening News*) made the first reference to it as such. On 21 March 1936 the *Daily Express Photonews* produced a drawing of a fort 325 ft deep with a normal main-line train running into it.

Having re-occupied the Rhineland, the Germans immediately set about constructing fortifications—a normal military precaution. Those early field works were destined to become the *Westwall*, which was known in the Anglo-Saxon world as the Siegfried Line, upon which we were going to hang out our washing. In the early stages of its development is was purely an army matter; it was not until the beginning of 1938 that Hitler succeeded in establishing party control over the General Staff. Egon Eis oversimplified the matter when he wrote, 'France had her line, and so Hitler had to have one too'.[24] The initial scheme was only a short line of works along the Saar river, but in 1938 Hitler, who later referred to himself as 'the greatest fortress builder of all time', conceived a vast programme of works running from the Swiss border to the Rhine on the Dutch frontier.

At this stage it is worth saying something about the *Westwall*, as it too had a role to play in the propaganda war during the late 1930s. Serious work started in May 1938, as a prelude to action against the Czechs. At that time the German armies had not achieved their full expansion and Hitler still imagined that action in the east would provoke the French into attacking in the west, as she was obliged to do under the terms of her treaty obligations. Thus the German works were designed to absorb any action along the French frontier while the main army delivered the *coup de grace* in the east.

As in the case of the Maginot Line, there were two walls—the actual one and the propaganda one. The former did exist and has often been compared to its French counterpart. However, except for the fact that they were both linear defence systems, the two had little in common. From the strategic point of view the Maginot Line was purely defensive, and being comparatively narrow in depth, once penetrated, was rendered ineffective. The *Westwall* consisted of an initial line, referred to as the army zone, which was anything up to 30 km deep, and double that in places, stretching the entire 560 km of Germany's western border. The design owed much to German trench war experience, where they had pioneered the use of integrated concrete strongpoints and a weakly held front line. Any attacker would be lured into successively stronger defences until he became bogged down. Behind the army zone was the air defence zone, designed to stop aircraft penetrating into the heart of the country.[25]

Thus the *Westwall* was a skeleton around which armies could manoeuvre, ready to strike when the enemy had become enmeshed in the defensive position. This consisted basically of a large number of bunkers arranged in a cluster pattern. Armed with anti-tank and automatic weapons, they could cover the obstacles in front with a broad pattern of fire, as well as providing mutual flanking protection within the cluster itself. The works were all small and were blended as far as possible into the terrain. Each was to a certain extent self-sufficient, although not on the scale of sophistication of the Maginot Line. There were no deep forts at all, in spite of what German propaganda tried to imply, and little use of armoured turrets. On the outbreak of war the defences were still incomplete. However, their loose structure, when garrisoned by a determined body of troops, was ideally suited to an improvised defence. Here, perhaps, was the realization of Pétain's 'battlefield prepared in peacetime'.

As if aware of the shortcomings of their *Westwall*, the German propaganda effort during 1938–40 was concentrated on selling it as the most formidable scheme of defence ever designed. Its purpose was declared to be to protect Germany from her aggressive neighbours, and it was given wide publicity with official encouragement. A number of 'inspired' books were allowed to be published, all of which stressed its defensive nature and exaggerated its strength, comparing it with the 'old-fashioned' Maginot Line. General von Rundstedt's biographer states that he laughed when he saw the *Westwall* for the first time.[26] Apart from printing the photographs of deep forts in the Czech defences, Rudolph Kühne stated in his book *Der Westwall* 'No enemy can approach this bulwark of steel and concrete unpunished. Even an attack with the strongest means will, despite the greatest sacrifice, collapse under the power of the defensive armament'. Referring to the Maginot Line, which he said had been built 'to quieten the French population', he said that its purpose was offensive, to act as a base of operations for a field army. Another author, writing in a similar vein, included a chapter entitled 'The Maginot Line, France's guilty conscience'.

Foreign correspondents were given guided tours and photographs were issued of blond-haired young 'volunteers' busy with pick and shovel working for the peaceful defence of the Fatherland to counter French aggression—something that was far from the minds of the French General Staff.

The other side, however, was not idle in the war of words. The issue of Belgian neutrality prompted a rash of speeches from high-ranking generals and politicians, all of which fostered the impression that Maginot-type works would be built on the northern frontier. Even writers of fiction got in on the act. In 1938 a film was made entitled *Double crime sur la Ligne Maginot*. This was basically a thriller, but had a hidden message to emphasize the power of the fortifications. The paradox, though, was that much of it was shot in the old German forts around Metz and Thionville. The same location was used for an American *March of Time* film which was issued in November 1938. In Vivien Rowe's book there is a photograph of a pre-1914 German turret battery of the Metz type which he states as being in the Maginot Line, and which he credits to *March of Time*. In November 1939, French newsreels showed the first interior shots of the Maginot forts. The Germans, however, were up to the same trick. They were digging out archive pictures of their old forts and handing them out as being of batteries in the *Westwall*.

In 1939 a book written under the pseudonym of Commandant Cazal appeared, entitled *La Guerre! Maginot, Siegfried; Roman de Demain*. In the same year Bernard Newman published a book under the title *Maginot Line Murder*; all good stirring stuff.

The rest of the pre-war literature on the subject was of the 'from an informed source' type. One of the classics was called *The Maginot Line— The Facts Revealed by a French Officer*, issued in England and 'authorized by the French War Office'. This includes one of the usual nonsensical cut-away drawings and repeats the old legend of some sort of super-tunnel that linked up all the forts. There was never any such thing. He also talks about anti-aircraft guns fitted into turrets that opened up. These, too, were a figment of the imagination.

Among the officially invited visitors to the Maginot Line before the war was Winston Churchill. He toured the Rhine defences in August 1939, and, although impressed by what he was shown, was deeply disturbed by the defensive attitude of the French officers he met.[27]

The myth of the wall of steel from the North Sea to Switzerland (or the Mediterranean, depending on which version was current at the time) was born partly of wishful thinking, which nobody in official circles did anything effective to counter. The more secrecy that prevailed, the more the rumours spread, until many in official circles believed them themselves. The Germans were not fooled, and were extremely well-informed about the Maginot Line, especially after the occupation of Czechoslovakia. In the captured archives there are detailed maps of the French north-eastern frontier, showing even the individual casemates and observation posts.

The French, however, swallowed the myth about the *Westwall*, which was extremely weakly garrisoned during the invasion of Poland. The half-hearted 'offensive' in the Saar area petered out after a few miles, and that was all the help that was given to the unfortunate Poles. The French army did not want to get tangled up in the German defences. Even as late as 1944 the myth continued to exercise its power. The Allied commanders were full of respect for the *Westwall* which, when it was finally encountered, proved to be hardly a formidable obstacle, as it had been designed to cope with the relatively small calibre weapons of 1939.

Chapter 7

Manning and organization for war

The highest command entity in the Maginot Line was the *Région Fortifiée* (RF), which was divided up into sectors. Each of these was commanded by a general officer who was responsible for both garrisons and interval units. The sectors were further divided into sub-sectors, each held by a regiment of fortress infantry with two or three battalions. Each *ouvrage* had an officer in overall command, with subordinate commanders for artillery, infantry and engineers. Like the captain of a warship, the fort commander was frequently likened to God![28]

In addition, the artillery had a subsidiary command structure, in that the firepower of two or three forts was linked together to form an artillery group, which came under the control of the artillery commander of the sub-sector. The purpose of this was to enable a fort to be supported by its neighbours, and for massed battery fire to be easily coordinated. It also ensured a chain of communication between the forts and the heavier long-range guns of the interval troops.

The eyes of the defences were the observation posts; without them the garrisons were blind. These came in a variety of forms, and were to be found mounted integrally within the perimeter of a fort, outside on some prominent feature or on one of the interval casemates. Normally, the posts were protected by armour-plated domes of several types, but some were in concrete emplacements. The domes, known as *cloches*, varied in thickness between 18 and 33 cm of metal and were in many ways the only parts of a Maginot work directly visible to an approaching enemy. For the overall defence to be effective, the observers had to be

An observation post high in the Alps overlooking one of the passes (Col de Restefond)

able to achieve 360 degree coverage, as well as being able to see into any area of otherwise dead ground where an enemy could assemble.

The basic artillery observation post consisted of a pair of domes mounted on the roof of a block. One was the so-called surveillance position which was manned by an officer equipped with powerful binoculars. His duty was constantly to scan the ground within his field of vision. He was connected by an acoustic tube to the neighbouring dome which was manned by an NCO. His mission was to register accurately any target spotted by the officer, and for this purpose had a 21 cm periscope in the roof. Although the lens was covered by a shutter when not in use, such instruments proved to be vulnerable to sniper fire.

In addition there were the auxiliary observation posts, where one man with a periscope combined the duties of target spotting and registration. The final version was for infantry purposes, to scan the outer surface of a fort or to cover an entrance block or casemate. These had three embrasures into which could be fitted episcopes, and in case of attack, automatic rifles and 50 mm mortars, the arrangement being left to the individual observer.

The various types of post were reached via a ladder from the interior of the block on which they were situated. They were fitted with a floor that could be raised or lowered to suit the size of the man on duty, a seat, and a light that could be dimmed. Two telephone circuits were provided (one in reserve), which ran directly to the artillery (or infantry) command post.

Fire control was an exact science, with its own complicated jargon. The following is a simplification of the course of events after a potential target had been spotted. The officer making the observation telephones the command post, giving the type of target (two tanks, enemy infantry concentration, etc), the position in relation to any prominent feature, and reading from the panoramic photograph in front of him, the rough bearing and elevation. His partner, the NCO in the neighbouring dome, hears this information through the acoustic tube, and with the use of his periscope, locates the target, works out the exact co-ordinates and passes them on to the command post.

There the first message is received by a telephonist, who writes the information on a blackboard. The staff work out the necessary details required by the artillery commander, whose duty it is to decide whether it is worth a shot.

Having decided that it is, he nominates the block or blocks to carry out the shoot, and the detailed information from the second observer is relayed to the block command post. There, range and elevation are computed and any necessary calculations for outside temperature, wind speed, etc. The block commander, having checked the details, then gives the orders for the number of rounds, type of shell and fuse setting. This is passed on to the gunlayers in the turrets by means of pointers revolving around a dial.

Signal dial for the transmission
of orders. Hackenberg, Block 9
(Kristensen)

When the alert is sounded, the gun details run to their positions, where the fire orders would already be appearing on the dials. The airlock is closed, the interior pressure mounts and the turret raised into its firing position. Far below, the necessary shells are taken from the racks and placed onto the hoists which brings them up to the firing chamber. There four men, two layers and two loaders, are cramped into the confined space under the curved roof, manning two 75 or 135 mm guns. The turret is traversed on to the target and the guns elevated. Shells are slammed into the breeches which are clanged shut. A muffled explosion, breeches are flung open and the next rounds go in, while the empty cases clatter away down the chute. It was reckoned that a twin 75 mm turret was worth eight similar field guns, and could get off some 24 rounds per minute. It has also been calculated that the largest fort, Hackenberg, with all guns firing, could deliver 4 tons of shells per minute.

Once the shoot was finished, the observers reported the effect of the fire. The job of observer was the most unenviable in the whole system. Specially alert men who were not prone to excessive imagination were chosen, but in spite of this they had to be regularly relieved. The worst

Three-tier bunks in the troop accommodation at the small Immerhof *ouvrage*. Above each bunk is a small shelf. Note the sheet steel lining of the casemate (Kristensen)

problem was the cold, for the openings in the domes in which they sat were the main exits for the used air, which whistled past their ears under pressure. In spite of sheepskin coats, they suffered from excessive cold, and the noise of rushing air made them unable to hear. This in turn led to a sense of isolation, as observation is often a combination of several senses. Unable to hear or smell, they could only rely on their eyes. In addition, they were the only members of the garrison to be directly subjected to enemy fire. The domes were an easy target and proved particularly vulnerable to the high velocity 88 mm guns, as well as to accurate sniper fire. Even if the shells did not penetrate, the noise of impact would have been enough to demoralize the most phlegmatic soldier.

The gun crews were organized like the rest of the garrisons, into a three-watch system—duty, stand-by and rest. The first two categories formed the combat personnel; the stand-by crew joined those on duty when the alert sounded. Apparently the tendency was for as many men as possible to try and stay out at their blocks instead of marching back to the barracks for their rest periods; they got fed up with carting their kit to and fro, and wanted to avoid the inevitable fatigues. However, when the forts did come under fire, they were only too glad to get away to the rear. The barracks were often the only place to get uninterrupted sleep well away from the noise of almost constant firing.

The officers were in many ways less fortunate; they had no reliefs. During long periods of combat they were on duty day and night. A really sustained attack could have led to vital members of the garrison simply dropping from fatigue.

The only people to have any privacy in a Maginot fort were the commanding officer and the block commanders, who merited single rooms. These were fitted with a bed, cupboard, chair and table, all metal, and a wash basin. There were no refinements such as luxuriously appointed officers' messes.

In the main command post were housed the separate artillery and infantry posts, the fort commander's post and the main telephone exchange with two main circuits. One was available for the orders of the commanding officer and the other was for communication between observers and artillery. In addition, there was an advanced first-aid room, toilets and rooms for the staff.

The infantry command post was responsible for co-ordinating the defence of the infantry blocks and controlling the fire of their numerous weapons. In the same way as the artillery, the observers were connected to the intelligence section in the post, whose duty it was to feed the commander with information. He made the decision whether or not to open fire and with which weapons. He was also responsible for the interior defence of the fort if the enemy succeeded in getting inside.

The commanding officer of the whole fort received information from both artillery and infantry which was passed on to his own intelligence staff. There the log was kept which noted all orders given and the time, just like the log of a warship. He had overall control of the battle and was in direct communication with the interval troops and the sub-sector headquarters.

In addition to the telephone network, each fort was equipped with radio. This proved, however, to be of little practical value, as all messages had to be encoded and decoded, which took far too much time for urgent communications. Another disadvantage was that the antennae proved highly vulnerable, usually being slung from metal frames along the back of the entrance blocks. The most powerful transmitters only had a range of 25 km.

The external telephone network, however, was extremely sophisticated. The circuits were well buried underground, 2 m deep, and the cables were encased in lead. All various outside parts—casemates, infantry shelters and field observation posts—were connected up to the forts, which in turn had lines into the civilian network. At various places on the surface there were junction boxes, housed in shell-proof concrete bunkers. Ground commanders could use these to tap into the system in an emergency, without the usual army problem of having to lay wires all over the place.

The most complicated part in any fort was the artillery command post. Its commander was not only responsible for the service of the fort's guns and the ammunition supply system, but also to the group commander in control of the overall fire pattern of the neighbouring works. The actual post was divided into two parts, the intelligence section and the fire control section. Incoming messages from the observers were logged in the intelligence section which had copies of the documents used by the former. These were laid out on a long table which was manned by clerks and several NCOs. Behind them stood an officer who verified the figures before passing them on to the commanding officer. He then selected the block or blocks to fire and passed the figures on to the fire control section for the necessary calculations to be made. It took between two and three minutes from the time of observation to opening fire, and the results were extremely

DIAGRAM OF ARTILLERY COMMAND POST ORGANIZATION

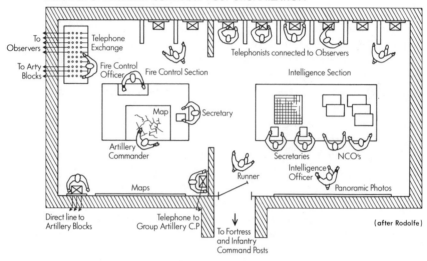

To Observers

To Arty Blocks

Telephone Exchange

Fire Control Officer

Fire Control Section

Telephonists connected to Observers

Intelligence Section

Map

Secretary

Artillery Commander

Secretaries

NCO's

Intelligence Officer

Runner

Panoramic Photos

Direct line to Artillery Blocks

Maps

Telephone to Group Artillery C.P.

To Fortress and Infantry Command Posts

(after Rodolfe)

accurate. The garrisons had used the frequent stand-by periods to work out the co-ordinates of any likely target, but the range of their guns was limited more or less to objectives within their own territory.

Apart from the regular troops housed in the peacetime barracks who were responsible for the care and maintenance of the defences, the garrisons would be supplemented by reservists on mobilization. In the case of a surprise attack, the regulars would immediately man the forts and then assimilate the reservists as they arrived. These mainly came from the surrounding districts and were known as *frontaliers*. They could be summoned for duty by siren, or if more time were available, by telegram. The purpose of this was to ensure swift mobilization of a vital part of the *couverture* in that the reservists did not first have to travel to distant regimental depots. Psychologically, such men, given the usual strong provincial loyalties of the French, had a vested interest in the defence of their homes and property. They arrived at their places of duty in civilian clothes and were kitted out on the spot. The pervading damp of the forts had the disadvantage that, in time, the kit stored there tended to deteriorate.

The Maginot Line was occupied for the first time in 1936. Lt-Colonel Rodolphe, who was the artillery group commander of the *ouvrages* around Hochwald in the Lauter RF, described the works at the time as being unfinished, dripping with water, unheated and sparsely lit. He goes on to say, however, that such conditions were borne with good humour. The garrisons soon came to regard themselves as elite units, which was helped by the fact that every man was in some ways a specialist and had a distinct job to do. He was an expert and could take a pride in himself and in his work; there were no underemployed troops who had somehow to be made to 'look busy'.

After the Rhineland crisis was over the reservists were sent home. The permanent garrisons could then settle down to some serious training, their lot relieved by being able to move their wives and families into quarters. As the Maginot Line was a totally new concept, there were few precedents for such an organization and everything had to be worked out from scratch. If a shooting war had started in 1936, the performance of the Line would have been woefully inadequate. As the frontier areas were still populated, live firing and testing of the guns was impossible and practical work had to be carried out elsewhere. A part of the Line, to the north of Bitche, was in a military training area, and it was there that the garrisons were sent one by one, for a week of intensive working up.

During 1937 the various systems were perfected and the photographs and diagrams for the observers were made up. Armies being the same everywhere, great care was devoted to the production of handbooks for everything concerning the operation of the defences. 'Standing orders' proliferated and had to be learned both by the regulars and by the reservists who attended for their annual training. It was during 1937 that many key men were sent off to the navy to study the organization on board a warship. Also, the ground in front of the forts was studied and measured in minute detail.

By 1938 the whole of the Maginot Line was in full working order in theory at least. From March to May it was again on a full war footing on the occasion of the occupation of Austria. In September came the Czechoslovak crisis and a further recall of the reservists. There was apparently some irritation among the *frontaliers* at being once again dragged away from their homes, and a few of them arrived for duty rolling drunk. On the whole the French part-mobilization was catastrophic, but the units of the Maginot Line were quickly ready for action.

Some token efforts were made at the time to increase the comfort of the troops in the forts, but in reality little was done. This can perhaps be explained by the gulf between officers and men that existed in the French army at the time, as well as the low pay and lack of prestige. A

Czech officer who visited the Line after it had surrendered made the following points: 'The designers, however, had given relatively little thought to the spiritual needs of the defenders ... As such a large fort cost so many million francs, surely it would have been worthwhile to add a few thousand to create a comfortable atmosphere in the soldiers' accommodation and rest rooms?' He goes on to suggest that the barrack rooms should have had the walls and ceilings painted, should have had pictures hung on the walls and been provided with decent floor coverings. All his suggestions, and there were many of them, would be obvious to any commanding officer today. The author of the above remarks was full of National Socialist ideology, which was obsessed with such things as the value of healthy sport and moral instruction.[29] The bulk of the German forces had an ideology, but the French had none.

It must be remembered that the bulk of the men were living in the forts for the best part of a year. They did have leave and were able to walk about outside, but if one visits a fort today one finds it hard to imagine living under such primitive conditions for so long. However, to judge by the performance of the garrisons in combat, the lack of creature comforts did not materially impair their efficiency or morale.

The final call-up came in the spring of 1939, when Germany absorbed the rump of Czechoslovakia, and from then until the surrender in June, 1940, the Maginot Line was on permanent alert. Some of the married men were released initially, but for the rest, it was a ceaseless round of duty, the occasional period of leave, and, as in fortresses anywhere, the battle against boredom.

Chapter 8

The phoney war

On 2 September 1939, France ordered general mobilization and the following day war was declared. Until May there followed the period known as the Phoney War—the French called it *la drôle de guerre*. It is only proposed to give an account of the Battle of France in so far as it affected the Maginot Line. For an excellent study of the subject, one cannot do better than read Alistair Horne's *To Lose a Battle*. The role of the Maginot Line, in fact, was marginal to the events of 1939–40, but has to be understood within the framework of the final battle itself.

The Line was put on a full war footing on 24 August, before general mobilization, when the reservists who had previously been released and the men on leave were recalled. The following day the wives and children were evacuated from the rear camps; according to one source they were only allowed 30 kg of baggage each.[30] The general feeling among the garrisons was, however, that another Munich would intervene and that the families would soon be back. Once hostilities had been declared the whole area in front of the fortifications was designated a prohibited zone. All the inhabitants were evacuated, leaving the farm animals to roam about. The interval troops moved in, and by all accounts the mobilization went fairly smoothly. It did, however, mean that the vital armament industries were robbed of key personnel.

The Allies went to war over Poland, so something had to be done to help that unfortunate people, bravely fighting against the German Panzer divisions. As far back as the Czech crisis in 1938, an agreement existed whereby France would launch an attack in the west if Poland were invaded. To judge by statements made at the time, the French High Command had no intention of doing anything really active, so deeply ingrained was the defensive mentality. This could best be summed up by harking back to the words of General Maurin, who, when he was War Minister in 1935, asked 'How can we still believe in the offensive when we have spent thousands of millions to establish a fortified barrier? Would we be mad enough to advance beyond this barrier upon goodness knows what adventures?'[31] The mentality behind French strategic thinking in 1939 is today almost impossible to comprehend. Sixty-seven French divisions, faced by a skeleton force of nineteen weak German ones, without armour, sat and did virtually nothing.

What they did was to undertake the so-called Saar offensive. On 7 September nine French divisions advanced from the Maginot Line into the Saarland, accompanied by excited press coverage. By the 12th they had progressed some 5 miles on a 16-mile front and had occupied a handful of villages. No attempt was made to pierce the thinly held *Westwall*, and when Poland capitulated it was decided to pull back behind the fortifications. By 4 October the withdrawal was complete. The German generals, who had been terrified by the thought of a large-scale offensive in the west while their troops were committed in Poland, breathed a sigh of relief, and amazement. Once again the bluff had worked. The French High Command, aware of their (imagined) material disadvantage, believed that time was on their side. They only had to wait until the full Allied potential had been built up in order to wage the time-honoured war of attrition. It was not considered that anything much could be undertaken before 1941!

The arrest of the offensive was to have a disastrous result on the morale of the French army. The blowing of the Rhine bridges indicated that there was no longer any intention of offensive action and the watchword became '*Pas d'histoires, pas des provocations, pas de bruit*'. Freely translated this meant don't go looking for trouble, don't provoke the enemy, don't make a noise.

The above applied to the forts themselves. On 3 September the artillery group commander of the Hochwald forts was informed by the CO of the sub-sector, 'The state of war is unconfirmed. Avoid frontier incidents. Don't cross the border, but if the enemy penetrates to our side, chase him off with small-arms fire'. It was not until the 6th that the state of war was confirmed, but the forts were forbidden to open fire without the permission of the sector commander. In this respect it should be remembered that hardly any of the guns had ever been tested. The permanent crews had had some live firing practice, but not on the weapons that they would have to operate in war.[32]

On 9 September a regiment of interval troops undertook a raid on a German frontier village, and one of the 75 mm turrets at Hochwald (the only one that could reach over the border) was authorized to fire a few rounds in support. After a few shots one of the two guns went out of action, which caused some consternation. It was subsequently discovered that the fault was caused by defective ammunition. It seems that the intention was to use up old stocks in the forts. Luckily it was decided to sort through all the ammunition and discard suspect items. The incident, however, did result in permission being given to test the other turrets. According to Rodolphe, 'The Boche remained indifferent and our petty manifestations did not trouble them'.

In the meantime there were frequent changes of interval troop units, and each new commanding officer promptly changed the established routine, without bothering to consider that the fort garrisons had better knowledge of the terrain that they covered. This situation was partly resolved when 12th Army Group succeeded in establishing its authority over all units in its area. General Prételat's Army Group covered the frontier from Thionville to Saverne in the Vosges, so he still only controlled the part of the Metz RF east of the Moselle, and the Rhine defences to the north of Saverne. Although this command set-up did not affect the final performance of the Line, it was typical of the poor planning which prevailed right from the outset. When the time came for the Maginot Line to fight, the ground commands had all disintegrated anyway.

As far as the special 'dispositions' that had been prescribed for the Ardennes were concerned, the defences along the Meuse at the beginning of the war consisted of some 40 pill-boxes armed with either a pair of machine-guns or one machine-gun and a small anti-tank weapon, designed to withstand the impact of shells up to 105 mm. It was not until November that a programme was initiated to increase the number of positions, but by the time the necessary material had arrived in January, it was too cold to pour concrete. Indeed, the bitter winter of 1939–40 imposed delays on construction work all along the front. By 10 May only 54 out of a projected total of 100 bunkers had been built, but they had not been fitted with their metal parts. The embrasures had to be protected by sandbags instead of armoured shields. Anti-tank ditches were too shallow, barbed wire was improperly anchored and many of the mines that had been laid had suffered from damp.[33]

If there was no active war, a propaganda offensive was being waged with some intensity, and the Germans were winning hands down. Their efforts were largely directed towards instilling a sense of security into the French. 'You remain in the Maginot Line and we will remain in the *Westwall*', was a sentiment heartily applauded by French popular opinion. Along the course of the Rhine both sides were within view of each other. The line of casemates had no offensive capability, and the interval troops were forbidden to fire their field guns. Train after train of German coal destined for Italy ran south along the river bank under the noses of the French gunners. 'Open fire on the German working parties? The Germans would only respond by firing on ours,' General Gamelin is reported to have said.

William Shirer travelled by train from Karlsruhe to Basle on 10 October and noted in his diary,

No sign of war, and the train crew told me not a shot had been fired on this front ... We could see the French bunkers and at many places great mats behind which the French were building fortifications. Identical picture on the German side. The troops appeared to be observing an armistice. They went about their business in full sight and range of one another ... Queer kind of war.

He also says that he observed German soldiers cheering a football match that was in progress over the water in France. A catch phrase at the time was that the enemy were *pas méchants*.[34]

Another ploy used by the Germans was to encourage hatred of the British by constantly harping on the puny number of troops that it was able to contribute. This theme was spread by means of dropped leaflets and music programmes piped from loudspeakers across the frontier. A certain Paul Ferdonnet became the French equivalent of 'Lord Haw Haw', but there is some evidence that his broadcasts were taken seriously. On both sides of the Rhine large hoardings covered with slogans were constructed, which neither side made any attempt to interfere with. General Spears tells the story of one such hoarding installed by the Germans, telling the soldiers of the 'Northern Provinces' that the British soldiery were sleeping with their wives and raping their daughters. The French unit opposite replied, 'We don't give a bugger, we're from the south.'[35]

The main part of the Maginot Line came to be known as *le trou* during the Phoney War. Apart from routine duties, most of its inhabitants spent as much time as possible trying to improve the sparse comfort of their lives, efforts which depended to a large extent on the goodwill of their commanding officers. The Line became fashionable, to the extent that it was extolled via the press and the cinema to the French populace.

Important visitors were constantly being shown around, including the Duke of Windsor who went to Hochwald at the end of October. His trip provided copy for journalists who had nothing else to write about. While he was there a few shots were loosed off into no-man's-land for his benefit. General Beaufré, at the time a junior staff officer, was sent to escort a VIP to Lorraine, and on his return commented, 'The army is rotting from inaction'.[36]

During November it was observed that the enemy had sent out a large working party that was impudently installing barbed-wire and mines right under the noses of the guns of the Hochwald forts. They were dispersed by 30 accurate rounds, but the artillery group commander was reprimanded for believing that he was at war.

Christmas came and went. Midnight Mass was celebrated in the main gallery at Hochwald, and the service was filmed for general distribution through the newsreels—Christmas in the Maginot Line. Amateur variety shows were performed and some of the forts organized bands. Still on a musical note, the late George Formby had a hit in England with a little ditty that went:

Imagine me on the Maginot Line
Sitting on a mine on the Maginot Line.

With the coming of the New Year activity increased slightly. The Germans patrolled the frontier areas, their presence betrayed by footprints in the snow. In an effort to combat boredom and to encourage the more adventurous spirits in the forts, *groupes francs* were formed. These were bands of volunteers who sallied out on offensive patrols, but, by and large, the Germans declined engagements.

Although the turret guns had been tested it was not until three months of war had passed that permission was finally given for the short-range guns to be fired. These were the 75 and 135 mm weapons in casemates and the 81 mm mortars, which were designed for use against an attack on the forts themselves. Owing to the virtual absence of anti-aircraft guns, German aircraft flew over the Maginot Line with impunity. Some efforts were made to fire box barrages with the 75 mm turret guns at maximum elevation, but these appear to have been ineffective, as the reconnaissance flights went on undisturbed.

The British Expeditionary Force, far away in the northern frontier, had little contact with the Maginot Line, although some units were transferred for service as interval troops. Any impressions that they may have had about the existence of fortifications on the Belgian frontier were dispelled on arrival, and most of the winter was spent in

constructing primitive field works. General Sir Alan Brooke, then a
corps commander, visited two forts in the Metz RF, and in his diary left
a valuable and pointed commentary. Welshtenberg, a large *ouvrage* to the
east of Thionville which he visited in December 1939, reminded him of

a battleship built on land, a masterpiece in its way, and there is no doubt that the
whole conception of the Maginot Line is a stroke of genius. And yet! It gives
me but little feeling of security, and I consider that the French would have done
better to invest the money in the shape of mobile defences such as more and
better aircraft and more heavy armoured divisions rather than to sink all this
money into the ground.

Two months later he was at Hackenberg, the largest of the Maginot
forts. This was the prime showpiece in the Metz RF, corresponding to
Hochwald in the Lauter RF. After commenting favourably on the
engineering aspects of the place, he noted,

Millions of money sunk into the ground for a purely static defence, and the total
fire-power developed by these works bears no relation to the time, work and
money spent in their construction. Their most dangerous aspect is the
psychological one; a false sense of security is engendered, a feeling of sitting
behind an impregnable iron fence; and should the fence perchance be broken,
the French fighting spirit might well be brought crumbling with it.[37]

As this was written on 6 February 1940, and not by a military historian
being wise after the event, its note of prophecy is astonishing. Prior to
the war, little had been done in British military circles to encourage
mobility, but it would seem that the lessons of Spain and Poland had at
least been absorbed by some field commanders. This was not the case in
France. General Beaufré pointed out that 'the example of Poland did
not seem to apply to us with our greater density of troops reinforced by
the Maginot Line'.[38]

The Phoney War ended on 10 May 1940. Until then in the Maginot
Line it had been business as usual, even while indications of imminent
attack in the west were multiplying. Morale and discipline remained
steady among the garrisons, who tended to live in a community isolated
from the rest of world events. In some forts the attack was greeted with
relief. At last, after all the waiting, they would be able to have a crack at
the *Boche*. They were, however, destined to be robbed of the chance, and
would have to wait in the wings as destiny passed them by, until, just
before the final curtain, they made their brief début. At no time did the
Germans even contemplate a serious assault on the Maginot Line. Right
from the outset all their plans were directed towards the Low Countries.

Chapter 9

The German viewpoint

Long before 1932 Hitler had dreamed of smashing France in one decisive battle. Once established in power and bolstered by his series of cheap victories, he was surprised when England and France went to war over the question of Poland. The awful possibility of war on two fronts caused consternation in German military circles, and during the autumn of 1939 there was a deep gulf between the General Staff and their supreme warlord, whose desire for an immediate offensive in the West struck them as being both premature and fraught with danger.

Much has been written about the German war plans for the invasion of France. However, it is worth considering them briefly in so far as they affected the Maginot Line. It is idle to speculate whether or not their plans might have been different if the French had not built the Line where they did. The Germans were extremely well informed about the defences and no army commander in his right mind would attack a fortified position frontally if he had a viable alternative. The violation of Belgian (and Dutch) neutrality was justified speciously by the Germans as having been forced upon them by the existence of the fortified barrier. This was to forget that France was not the only enemy. Hitler needed the Low Countries as a base for airfields to attack Britain and would have over-run Belgium anyway.

Immediately after the defeat of Poland the bulk of the German army was rushed back to the West to strengthen the weak divisions in the *Westwall*. It has long been a popular misconception to ascribe too much omnipotence to the German military machine. In fact all the different command authorities were at loggerheads with each other, even after the final plan of attack had been approved. True to the Hitlerian trust in improvisation there were no precise directives as to what would happen once the breakout had been achieved.

The German General Staff had long been aware of the problem posed by the Maginot Line, and as far back as 1935 had been considering ways and means of eliminating the fortifications, if necessary. In that year the army approached Messrs Krupp and made a tentative enquiry for a gun capable of penetrating the French works, according to what was known about them at the time. Krupps had many years of experience in the design of super-heavy ordnance, including the 42 cm mortar that had demolished the Belgian forts in 1914. In 1936 Hitler asked if anything had been decided about a new super-gun, but at that stage apparently, nothing concrete had been undertaken, for at the end of that year, Krupps went ahead on their own initiative. They came up with a monster of 80 cm calibre which was codenamed 'Dora'. This gun, however, was not ready for use in 1940, and its only known employment was at the siege of Sevastopol. Had it been ready in time, in all probability it would have succeeded in crushing the Maginot forts which were only designed to cope with shells up to 42 cm calibre.[39]

There is one isolated document that considers a direct attack against the Maginot Line, but this was never part of official policy. Dated 25 November 1938, (after Munich), it was prepared for staff talks with the Italians, and envisaged a knock-out blow in Alsace–Lorraine to eliminate France and thus deprive Britain of her main continental ally. This, however, was an isolated instance rather than a recurring theme.

The Polish government surrendered on 17 November 1939, and Hitler summoned the three heads of the respective armed forces. At that meeting he told them of his decision to attack in the west via Belgium and Holland as soon as possible, and sent them away to draw up plans. His decision provoked a storm of protest. All three army group commanders, Rundstedt, Leeb and Bock, felt that such an attack had little prospect of success, and in this they were supported by Halder, the army chief-of-staff. However, on 9 October they were curtly informed by Hitler that he had decided that the attack would start on 25 November. This resulted in the first OKH (Army High Command) plan which carried the codename *Fall Gelb* (Case Yellow) and proposed merely a movement in the direction of Ghent, to separate the BEF from the French. It was uninspiring and reflected the hesitations of the staff concerned. Hitler had other ideas and sent it back for revision.[40]

It is unnecessary here to follow all the twists and turns of *Gelb*. There were frequent postponements and much acrimony in the background.

A mock-up of a Maginot casemate built by the Germans in 1939/40 at the Heuberg troop-training area. The turrets were made from sheet metal

Various Germans have claimed the authorship of the final plan, but it was in fact a combination of ideas dictated, to a certain extent, by circumstances. During the Autumn of 1939 Hitler had mentioned Sedan at a conference, and Manstein, at the time Rundstedt's chief-of-staff, certainly dreamed up the strong armoured thrust in the centre, between Dinant and Sedan along the Meuse. What finally emerged was a variant of *Gelb*, known as *Sichelschnitt*—the cut of the sickle. There were still the three army groups—Bock's Army Group B in the north, facing Holland and northern Belgium; Rundstedt's Group A concentrated in the centre with virtually all the panzer divisions; and Leeb's Group C stretched between Luxembourg and Switzerland. Bock and Leeb were to have subsidiary roles, albeit important ones. The former was, to employ Liddell-Hart's simile, a matador's cloak to entice the main Franco-British force into the Low Countries (they did not need much persuasion), by giving the impression that the main blow would fall there. Leeb's two armies were to keep up pressure on the Maginot Line and to stop the French removing the interval troops for use as reserves for the threatened sector. In the centre Rundstedt would strike a concentrated blow with seven armoured divisions through the 'impenetrable' Ardennes. Once the breakthrough had been achieved the French would still be left guessing which direction it would take—to the Channel, to Paris, or to the east to roll up the Maginot Line. Hitler had once boasted, 'I shall manoeuvre France right out of the Maginot Line without losing a single soldier'. This was somewhat of an exaggeration, but in effect, German losses were minimal in relation to the success achieved. 'Our plan', Halder told Hitler, 'must be to get behind the fortified line in northern France at the very start'.

Thus, the punch would brush past the shoulder of the Maginot Line where it ended at the weak extension around Montmédy, and would hit the incomplete bunkers along the Meuse, whose condition has already been mentioned. The Germans were fully aware of the inadequate nature of the defences there, and experience in Poland had taught them that tank guns and high velocity 88 mm weapons could easily deal with simple bunkers. A final refinement was that the attack would arrive neatly on the boundary of two French armies—General Corap's 9th and General Huntziger's 2nd.

Leeb's Army Group C comprised two armies—von Witzleben's 1st, whose 15 divisions covered the main part of the Maginot Line in the north-east, and Dollman's 7th army along the Rhine, with only four divisions. A total of 19 non-elite divisions was all that the Maginot Line was worth in German eyes. During the waiting period some thought was given to a subsidiary attack (codename *Fall Grün*—Case Green) against the Line in the Saar area on the assumption that the main assault would be successful and the French badly weakened. This never got off the ground, and Leeb was confined to the role of spoiling attacks and demonstrations to hold as many French troops as possible in the fortified zone. The possibility of an attack in the area was one that was assiduously leaked. In April, French intelligence picked up the report of a speech by Goering in which he stated that an attack was planned for two points against the Maginot Line between 3 and 15 May, and that the Germans were prepared to lose 500,000 men and 80 per cent of the *Luftwaffe*.

Another plan that was considered was given the codename *braun* (brown). This envisaged an attack towards the Langres plateau via the Belfort Gap, and was first discussed by Hitler on 21 March. It was basically an alternative to *grün* and was to be carried out with the support of a number of Italian divisions. It assumed that 30-plus divisions would be available and that any French reserves would be fully occupied on the main front. This would have had the effect of turning the extreme south of the Maginot Line by penetrating the weak Rhine defences and attacking the rear of the main French armies. Preparation was to be only on paper until the main attack was under way, and its implementation would depend on the success of the latter. Assuming delays in Italian mobilization, it was felt that six weeks after the start of *gelb*, a strike could be made across the Upper Rhine.

However, there was little serious intent behind *braun*. Mussolini had no intention of declaring war until France had been decisively beaten, and if that was the case, the Germans would hardly need Italian troops on the Rhine. During March Leeb was planning a number of assault crossings of the Rhine to the south of Strasbourg and there was some liaison with the Italians. But in the end *braun* was shelved, and the Italians only made a feeble demonstration in the south.

It is now known that the French had plenty of warning of German intentions, including a warning from their Military Attaché in Berne that the attack would begin between 8 and 10 May with Sedan as the main axis of movement. They had a pretty complete picture of the enemy order of battle and the concentration of the armoured divisions around Trier. All this mass of evidence was available to Gamelin, the French C–in–C, but he remained unconvinced. To the bitter end he believed that Leeb's Army Group had twice the number of divisions that it actually had.

The French were equally convinced that their defences around Sedan were adequate and that they could stop any attack there—in line with the old Pétain doctrine of hitting the enemy when he emerged from the woods. The lessons of Spain and Poland were totally ignored—the terrible combination of tanks and Stuka dive bombers. Gamelin could never forget the possibility of an attack on the Maginot Line or an outflanking movement through Switzerland. Later, in his memoirs he tried to justify the concentration of forces in the Line by remarking, 'Its existence alone guaranteed us, in the spring of 1940, that, at the moment when the Germans attacked via Luxembourg, Belgium and Holland, they could not at the same time make a decisive effort between Longuyon and Switzerland.' Such an intention never even entered Hitler's head.

Thus the Maginot Line garrisons were left to wither on the vine, becoming known as the forgotten army. Their knowledge of outside events was largely gained from the over-optimistic reports that they heard on the radio, and only slowly did the reality of the total nature of the defeat dawn on them. They went about their duties in a vacuum, devoted to seeing that no penetration took place on their front. All they saw during the first few days of the attack were numerous German aircraft, on their way elsewhere.

Chapter 10

The Battle of France
first phase

The German attack in the west on 10 May 1940 opened with the whole of the *Luftwaffe* in action and an advance into Belgium and Holland, accompanied by a number of special operations.[41] One of these was the capture of the key Belgian fort of Eben Emäel by a picked force of airborne commandos who were landed by glider on top of the fort. There, they demolished the turrets and casemates one by one, and at the same time blew in the ventilation shafts, using a new form of hollow charge that had been tested against the Czech fortifications. Eben Emäel was situated to the north of Liege where the Albert Canal joins the Meuse. Its rapid elimination was vital in order to secure bridges across the canal.

That particular fort, however, cannot be compared to the Maginot Line. It was one of three which the Belgians had built in the inter-war period in advance of Liege, in order to try and update the pre-1914 defences. Eben Emäel was too far away from its neighbour to receive supporting fire, so the Germans could operate more or less undisturbed. Such an attack would not have worked against a part of the main Maginot Line, as all the forts there were integrated into an overall fire pattern. Any enemy activity on top of one would have led to a rain of shells from all directions.

In the Maginot Line itself, nothing much happened on that first or on subsequent days. Moving out from the defences to the west of the Moselle in the Metz RF, according to plan, a light cavalry division came up against strong German armoured forces moving west through

Luxembourg. The French withdrew and no further attempt was made to disturb the enemy build-up when it was at its most vulnerable. It was then that the Maginot Line had its real chance to play a decisive role. Acting as a secure base, it could have supported a strong move into Luxembourg to smash the frail German flank and upset their entire programme. Even after the breakthrough had been achieved, Gamelin was convinced that it was a feint and that the main battle would be fought in Belgium, where Bock was busily flapping his matador's cloak.

On the second day the only enemy activity noted was in the air. However, the first losses were incurred when a train on the narrow gauge railway near Hagenau, bringing men back from leave, was bombed. Several were killed and wounded. Interval troops holding the salient around Longwy were attacked and withdrew. German activity, such as it was, was concentrated on the western part of the defences in those early days, as they were obviously aware of the danger to their flanks. The leading panzer columns were already through the weak Belgian frontier fortifications, and were racing for Bouillon. The German news bulletins were concentrating on affairs in the north, ignoring what was afoot in the Ardennes.

12 May was characterized by more general pressure along the whole of the Maginot Line, which strengthened Gamelin's belief in the possibility of a serious attack. Fighting continued in the Longwy salient, where the French made a further withdrawal. In the east an advance observation post was lost to a determined infantry assault, in spite of intervention by one of the turrets of the Four-à-Chaux *ouvrage* which fired 500 rounds.[42]

The fourth day of the attack was the crucial one, when Guderian's troops managed to cross the Meuse at Sedan. The bunkers there, although some of them put up a token defence, were mostly reduced by the preliminary Stuka bombardment and by shells fired across the river. Those that survived managed to inflict losses on the troops crossing the river in inflatable assault boats, but were finally eliminated by determined shock troops, equipped with explosives, grenades and flame-throwers. Many of the defenders had been so demoralized by the dive-bombers that they surrendered without a fight. German pressure continued in the Longwy area and, as the breach at Sedan widened, the French troops to the east of it were pressed back on to the end of the Maginot Line. General Prételat, the army group commander, was convinced that the next step would be an attack on the rear of the Line, and began to move forces to his threatened left wing.

For the first time the Maginot Line in the Metz RF to the east of the Moselle was attacked, but the fortress artillery was able to repel the enemy with ease. Further to the east there were more incursions into the Lauter RF. Prételat issued orders that losses were not to be incurred in defending unimportant posts in advance of the Line, and that interval troops were to retire and not attempt to recapture them.

Thus, by the end of the fourth day, the Maginot Line had already been outflanked to the west and had lost its one great opportunity to smash the German attack before it developed. Had the fortifications been used properly by the High Command, the course of history could well have been altered. As it was, the enemy had the initiative, the sacred soil of France had once again been violated, and that which the Maginot Line was designed to prevent had happened. From then on its garrisons were condemned to impotence as the whole of the French grand strategy lay in ruins.

On 14 May the probing attacks continued against the Line, while the breach was extended to a width of some 65 km. Far to the east, locked up inside the Hochwald fort, the artillery group commander noted, 'This day could be considered the first day of battle for the sector'. However, the garrison had time to entertain a visitor—an American journalist by the name of Dorothy Thompson. The sight of a woman was a welcome relief for the monastic community, and she was permitted to fire a gun from one of the 75 mm turrets. For this she was awarded the honorary rank of Gunner 1st Class and given the insignia of Fortress Artillery Group No 3.

In spite of such diversions, the sector around Hochwald was very busy, having at last been given permission to fire at will! A large number of rounds were loosed off, both from the turrets and from a battery of ancient 120 mm field guns which had been emplaced on top of the fort. Originally these had been installed to give some firing practice to the otherwise idle 81 mm mortar and casemate crews, but the ancient weapons were to prove extremely useful, on account of their comparatively long range. Rodolphe noted in his diary, 'We have seen the enemy at last'. By this he meant direct observation from the forts of German infantry who had crossed the River Lauter and driven in some of the advance posts. During that evening the first German 'heavy' guns came into action against the Maginot Line, when some shells from a 280 mm railway gun were fired at Hochwald and Schoenenbourg. Becoming worried that enemy artillery fire might interrupt ammunition supply from the rear, the group commander asked for reserves to be brought in as there was sufficient room in the magazines. He also demanded a reconnaissance flight to try to determine the position of the 280 mm gun, but Corps replied that the only aeroplane that they owned had been shot down near Strasbourg that morning.

The sixth day heralded developments that would later have grave consequences for the reputation of the Maginot Line. To the west attacks on the Longwy salient continued. Held by General Condé's 3rd Army, this was the pivot around which the defeated 2nd Army was retreating from Sedan. This did have the effect of slowing the outflanking movement of the Line, but by then there were no reserves to plug the breach. If the 2nd Army disintegrated, Condé himself would be threatened. On his own initiative he reinforced the endangered front with two divisions.

During 14–15 May, the left flank of the German troops in the breakthrough had arrived in the general area of Carignan and Villy, where they were the first to come up against CORF-type fortifications, albeit in the comparatively weak Montmédy bridgehead, and they managed to cross the small Chiers river. In the extreme east of the Lauter RF the forts were again shelled by the 280 mm railway gun, which although it did no damage, left enormous craters on the surface. General Gamelin, isolated in his distant HQ at Vincennes, still continued to believe in an imminent assault through Switzerland. What reserves there were being sent to Huntziger's already shattered 2nd Army, as it was assumed that the Germans would wheel to the east behind the Maginot Line.

'We are in the open now', wrote General Guderian on the 16th[43], and by the end of the day his divisions were over the Serre and not far from Laon. Rommel, too, was into France and moving west towards Avesnes. There, the frontier fortifications, such as they were, had been constructed imperfectly the previous winter, and only consisted of a few bunkers backed up by barbed-wire. Oddly enough, Rommel seems to have been a victim of pre-war propaganda, for he believed that he was up against the 'Maginot Line'. He detailed a plan for a set-piece attack against the fortifications to his superior, von Kluge. Rommel, as usual, commanded from one of the leading tanks, and described actions against the bunkers which cost him a few men and tanks. That night he wrote in his diary, 'The way to the west was now open ... We were through the Maginot Line.'[44]

Although the panzer divisions had already been committed to move towards the coast there was panic in Paris, as it was assumed that the thrust was aimed at the capital. The reinforcement of the 2nd Army had, for the moment, stopped the threat to the rear of the Maginot Line. However, in the area to the west of the Montmédy bridgehead, German units had infiltrated into some woods near the small work known to them as 505, commonly referred to as La Ferté, after the neighbouring village. The fort kept them pinned down by fire from its machine-guns. It was the work to the extreme left of the CORF line that had been built around Montmédy facing towards the Belgian frontier. It had originally been proposed to extend the line further to the west, but nothing had been done, largely on account of lack of money. As already mentioned, it was one of the *nouveaux fronts*, and as such, had hardly any integral turret artillery (there was one pair of 75s in the whole bridgehead).

In the east, Rodolphe noted, 'The day is calm. the enemy seems to have suspended its attack.' All along the length of the Maginot Line, the interval troops were pulling back from the advance posts and retiring under the guns of the forts. Along the Rhine both sides continued to stare at each other.

On the 17th, the eighth day of the attack, the first divisions of interval troops were withdrawn to form a new army (7th) whose mission was to block the approaches to Paris. This was the first indication of a process that was to continue in stages right up to the end of the campaign, leaving the forts progressively more and more to their own devices. At La Ferté the Germans succeeded in capturing one of the surrounding hills, thus enclosing the small fort from three sides. Although heavily bombarded it continued to fire accurately in support of counter-attacks by Foreign Legion and Moroccan interval troops.

A legend has grown up about the action at La Ferté, and the affair has to be seen in its correct perspective.[45] Its final capture was greeted by German radio as a major triumph—a mighty Maginot Line fort had fallen to the victorious troops of the *Wehrmacht*. This was perhaps a hint to the French not to denude the Line of further interval troops. French reaction was naturally to belittle the loss of what was, in fact, a minor work which bore little resemblance to a real Maginot-type fort. The truth is somewhere in between. Most accounts state that as it was the extreme westerly work, its position was weak and it could not be protected by fire from its neighbours, which was not strictly true. The problem was the lack of artillery in the position, as the fort itself was not isolated. It consisted of two units (505 A and 505 B) joined together by an underground communication tunnel. To the west it was protected by a casemate, and to the east by another fort on the far side of the village of La Ferté. In addition, there was a battery of field guns in the immediate vicinity. The Germans afterwards claimed to have destroyed an artillery turret, but, although retractable, this contained only twin machine-guns. The armament consisted of the normal infantry weapons of machine-guns, automatic rifles and 50 mm mortars, and the total garrison of the two units was 240 officers and men (compared to 1,200 in the largest works).

On the morning of the 18th a small German infantry patrol, led by an NCO, advanced towards the fort, penetrated the obstacles, which had probably been churned up by the intensive artillery action, and arrived at the western infantry casemate. This they managed to capture by throwing charges through the open embrasures. The small garrison was taken prisoner, but when the Germans tried to advance further towards the western part of the fort, 505 B, they were driven off by the intensity of their own artillery bombardment.

In the meanwhile a certain Lieutenant Germer was creeping forward from the direction of Villey with a small unit of pioneers. They managed to get through the obstacles unobserved, as the forts were apparently blinded by smoke and dust from the heavy barrage that was covering them. The Germans were using a creeping barrage, and Germer and his men crept from crater to crater behind the advancing curtain of shells. The forts were still firing, but wildly, and Germer managed to crawl on top in the vicinity of a mixed weapon turret. This he silenced by throwing in a grenade, before moving to the rear of the machine-gun turret. This had no openings other than the barrels of the guns, but by placing a charge on the rim, Germer managed to jam it. Shortly afterwards, the only other turret stopped firing of its own accord. The whole attack lasted only 15 minutes, according to the Germans. The following day Germer was again in action, and managed to silence the neighbouring work, 505 A. On the 20th the French tried a counter-attack to recapture the fort but were driven off by concentrated artillery fire. In the meanwhile the Germans had penetrated through the rear entrance into 505 B, and initially found no trace of the occupants, although obvious demolitions had been carried out. The whole place was full of fumes, and only when the ventilation system had been restored did they manage to get down to the lower levels. There they found the bodies of 210 French soldiers, many of whom had first been wounded. All had died of asphyxiation as the ventilation had failed; the remaining members of the garrison could not be found. The commanding officer had shot himself, according to the German account.

Cloche GFM (mixed-weapon turret) at La Ferté. Note the damage caused by the impact of German 88 mm shells

Germer was celebrated as a hero, but even the Germans themselves praised the bravery of the garrison in not surrendering. This is perhaps proof of the high morale of the fortress troops, and a direct contrast to the rest of the French army which, at the time, was rapidly disintegrating. As a result of the loss of La Ferté, parts of the Montmédy bridgehead were voluntarily abandoned. At the same time, the remaining CORF works in the minor fronts around Maubeuge and Valenciennes were encircled, and one by one surrendered or were reduced.

Along the rest of the Line there was still little action. The Germans continued to probe for weak spots that could perhaps be exploited and to pin down as many troops in the area as possible. In this respect they were largely unsuccessful, as by 19 May many units had already been withdrawn behind the fortified area to form a general reserve. The forts were still firing steadily and taking a toll of the enemy, without suffering any losses themselves. Immune to air and artillery bombardment, their only news of the outside world came from the still optimistic radio broadcasts. On that day Rodolphe wrote, 'We began to feel that all was not well in the north, but the appointment of Weygand as C-in-C of the French armies reassured us somewhat.' (He replaced Gamelin who had been sacked.)

The twin MG turret at La Ferté damaged in the attack by Lieut. Germer

Also on the 19th Prételat's 12th Army Group, which had previously only been responsible for the troops on the Rhine as far as Sélestat, was given command of the remaining forces between there and the Swiss border. Still, there was a persistent belief in an attack through Switzerland. General Prételat discovered that the dam across the Rhine at Kembs was still intact, as nobody had given permission for it to be blown up.

On the following day the panzer divisions reached Amiens and Arras, and Guderian had pushed a small force as far as the Channel at Abbeville. The Allied forces were finally split, and those in the north had their backs to the sea. One direct result of this success was that Hitler personally called off the assault crossing of the Rhine that Leeb had been planning, apparently to avoid pointless casualties. During the following few days the Maginot Line was left in relative peace. There was little shelling and groups of the garrisons were allowed outside to bask in the warm spring sunshine. For most of the time there was little to be seen of the enemy, although the observers warily scanned the approaches to the forts, still in expectation of imminent attack.

As a further illustration of the isolation of the garrisons, on 22 May Rodolphe noted in his diary, 'We are hoping that the Belgian armies will attack the flank of the enemy salient and stop his westward progress.' On the 26th the *ouvrage* of Schoenenbourg suffered its first casualty. An observer was killed by the flying débris from his periscope when his turret was hit by a shell. This illustrates the weakness already referred to. The Germans had discovered the vulnerability of the periscopes, and the French themselves were aware of this well before the war. Tests were carried out during the 1938 manoeuvres, and afterwards the commander of the Haguenau sector had prophesied, 'The casemates will perish through their turrets in the same way that a pear rots from the stalk.' Following the accident at Schoenenbourg the engineers came up with various solutions to a problem that should have been resolved long before, but by then there was no longer time left for rectifications. There was time, however, to replenish the magazines of the forts which, in the north-east, was carried out during the nights of 27 and 28 May. In spite of the general collapse, the rear areas of the Maginot Line where the main dumps were situated, continued to function. Hochwald, for example, received over 33,000 rounds of 75 mm ammunition. Some of the forts, when they surrendered, were found to have more ammunition in stock than they had had at the start of the attack.

Operation Dynamo, the evacuation of the BEF from the Dunkirk area, got underway on 27 May. The German High Command then had to decide what to do; their success had exceeded all expectations. Instead of busying themselves with a follow-up invasion of England, all their forces were re-grouped for the final knock-out blow against France, which had already been beaten anyway. This final phase of the Battle of France was known by the codename *rot* (red).

Chapter 11

The Battle of France
second phase

As we have seen, the original plan for *Fall Gelb* did not envisage a collapse on such a scale and had been backed up by various alternatives, including subsidiary assaults on the Maginot Line. Planning for *rot* started when *gelb* was already well under way, and on 20 May (the day Guderian reached the coast) it was ready for presentation to Hitler. This time there was none of the acrimony that had accompanied the planning for the earlier operation, although there was some division of opinion as to where the emphasis should be placed—to the east or west of Paris—and whether or not to attempt a subsidiary thrust across the Rhine in the Belfort area to take the retreating French armies in the rear. The latter project had earlier been envisaged under the code name *braun*, with Italian participation, but had never been more than a paper exercise. Mussolini was still not ready to move.[46]

The 20 May plan for *rot* foresaw a main attack on the Somme/Aisne front, followed a few days later by an offensive with 15 divisions across the Upper Rhine, and another with 8 divisions on the Maginot Line opposite Saarbrücken. There, the Germans had picked the weaker *nouveau front* and the zone of inundations. By a quirk of nature there had been little rainfall that year and the water levels were extremely low.

Hitler had also been having thoughts on the matter, independently of OKH as usual, and he proposed attacks on either side of Paris, plus another against the Line, again in the Saar area. On 25 May a revised plan was presented with the main thrust east of Paris as Hitler had demanded. This would have had the effect of pushing the bulk of the remaining French forces back against the Line. Once this had been achieved and when the Germans were on the Moselle in the Toul area, the Rhine was to be crossed.

In the final version of the plan the latter was to be omitted in so far as the attack via the Belfort Gap was concerned. The target date for launching the attack was set for 5 June (the final day of the Dunkirk evacuation), and on the 15th Leeb was to attempt to break through the Maginot Line in the Saar area. For this he had the 24 divisions of General von Witzleben's 1st Army. A secondary thrust across the Rhine, aimed at Colmar, was to be made by General Dollman's 7th Army, reinforced by a Corps of four extra divisions.

At the start of the attack the Germans were poised on a front that ran from the mouth of the Somme, along that river and then the Aisne, until it reached the end of the Maginot Line in the Montmédy area. While the Germans had been regrouping, little had been happening to the forgotten army. Badly frightened by the loss of La Ferté, GQG sent out a message which recommended accurate fire by neighbouring forts. They also (falsely) informed the sector commanders that Eben Emäel had been captured by parachutists landing on the roof. To counter such an attack, commanding officers were ordered to post patrols on the top of the forts, and tanks were allotted for use in clearing the superstructures in case of attack. The Maginot Line was about all that France had left, and they were determined not to lose it. Sending tanks, however, was just another example of the way in which French armour was dispersed all over the place, instead of being concentrated where it could do the most damage. There was no shortage of volunteers for such outside patrols.

1 June—'The enemy is still calm' (Rodolphe), and was to remain so for several more days. The drain of the last interval troops continued as the French tried to build up some sort of cohesive front and to form a reserve. As far as the fortress troops were concerned, no withdrawal was to be made without the personal authority of the Commander-in-Chief. That which had cost so much money could not simply be abandoned, even if dictated by military logic.

Three days later there was an accident at Schoenenbourg, when one of the old 120 mm guns that had been emplaced on the roof burst. A faulty round split the barrel and eight men were wounded by splinters, one of them fatally. Indicative of the fact that the logistics were still functioning, the wounded men were promptly evacuated to an outside hospital. Meanwhile, an artillery captain, with great presence of mind, loaded and fired the other gun himself, thus restoring morale.

5 June was the twenty-seventh day of the Battle of France and the day on which the Germans launched their final assault. Leeb's forces continued to make demonstrations along the Maginot Line, and those defending the Rhine were aware of the fact that troops were massing across the water. Two days later a reconnaissance aircraft was shot down in the north-east corner of the defences by interval troops firing machine-guns. In reading the few accounts of action in the Maginot Line one cannot help but be aware of the general aggressive attitude of the troops; there are no hints of defeatism and moral collapse. Sitting well protected from the screaming Stukas and having suffered only nominal losses, the fort garrisons could well afford a sense of superiority. Although events had already left them behind, they felt that they could resist indefinitely.

On 10 June the Government left Paris and Mussolini finally declared war: 'I can't sit back and watch the fight. When the war is over and victory comes I shall be left empty handed.' What ensued was aptly described by Telford Taylor as 'low tragicomedy in the Alps'. The French had progressively weakened the Alpine front by withdrawing troops for use elsewhere. When hostilities opened they had three divisions of fortress troops and four of interval troops to face six Italian army corps (34 divisions). The French immediately carried out a number of vital demolitions in the passes, including the transalpine railway tunnel at Modane. For ten days, however, the Italians did nothing.

For Prételat, the commander of the army group directly concerned, the worry was that the front was still anchored to the Maginot Line at Montmédy, but it was stretched to breaking point and would snap at any minute. It seemed to him that it would be sensible to retire from the fortifications and try to form a new line in the south to cover Lyons. It was not until 12 June that authority was given, but the few remaining interval troops could not be immediately disengaged. The garrisons of the forts were to remain to cover the withdrawal, which would begin from the salient to the north of Thionville. Orders were sent to the forts for preparations to be made to demolish their vital working parts, which caused consternation among the officers concerned. Only those men who needed to know were told, but a start was made to burn the accumulation of paper from nine months of war. Oddly enough at that moment, the first deliveries of 125 mm short-barrelled guns for the turrets arrived. These had been on order since before the war, but by then there were no specialists available to mount them.

Devastation caused by German bombardment in 1940. These small observation turrets were extremely vulnerable to 88 mm shells

The decision to abandon the Line was overtaken by events. Guderian was speeding towards the Swiss frontier, cutting off the line of retreat proposed by Prételat, whose army group was compressed into a triangle running from Longuyon to the Rhine at Hagenau, and from there along the river to Switzerland.

On 14 June Witzleben's 1st Army launched its long-awaited attack on the front between Saaralbe and St Avold—the day that Paris was occupied. His forces hit the French XX Corps just as they were pulling back from the fortifications, but they managed to conduct a fighting retreat.[47] However, the combination of dive-bombers, tanks and determined infantry made short work of the thin line of casemates that covered the 'dry' zone of inundations. On the flanks, the forts around Téting and Wittring, on the Saar, held out. Fort Bambesch, just to the south of the village of Zimming, garrisoned by four officers and 100 men, resisted until the evening of the 20th, six days after being cut off. The spirited garrison even tried to set up machine-guns in the open to bolster their defence. Two kilometres to the north was Fort Kerfent, a slightly larger work. The full weight of German artillery was brought to bear, and after a turret was damaged, it too had to surrender. The Germans were full of admiration for the occupants of these two forts who were prepared to fight on even when their situation was hopeless.

The day after the attack on the Saar was started, four divisions crossed the Rhine at three points—Marckolsheim, Neuf Brisach and Rheinau. The weak bunkers on the river bank were mostly silenced by dive-bombers and artillery firing across the water, and those that continued to fire were eliminated by pioneers. A defect in design had left patches of dead ground behind the shingle banks that lined the edge of the river. Small parties of German infantry were able to shelter behind these and creep up on the bunkers unobserved. Their tactics were the same as at La Ferté, whereby small patrols managed to throw explosives and grenades through the embrasures. The Rhine defences caused little trouble to the Germans, and there is some evidence of casemates surrendering easily, while others held out for two or three days. This can perhaps be explained by the fact that they were manned by small numbers, isolated from each other. The *esprit de corps* of a large fort never had the opportunity to develop, and they had been demoralized by months of inactivity and the state of non-war. Within two days the Germans were through Colmar and into the Vosges, behind the back of Prételat's disintegrating army group.

The Germans by then were ready for the kill, and all along the Maginot Line attempts were being made to penetrate it. It would seem that many local commanders were determined to bag a fort and earn themselves a medal. The only full account of the last days of the Line is Rodolphe's diary, which makes fascinating reading. It is quite clear from this that the group of forts centred around Hochwald had no intention of surrendering. In fact they still lived in a cloud-cuckoo-land of optimism. On 16 June he noted on the occasion of the radio announcement of the formation of a Pétain ministry, 'We again believe in a miracle'. Some outposts were being driven in, but the turrets kept up their full rate of fire. Parties were sent out to forage for ammunition and field guns left behind by the interval troops. Anything that was capable of offensive fire was collected and manned by gunners drawn from the mortar and casemate crews. Fighting patrols were organized from among engineers and other spare troops. The following day they received the news that Pétain had asked for an armistice—news that filled them with 'consternation'. They had food for two months and ammunition for three weeks at full rate of fire (Hochwald was firing an average of 2,000 rounds per day). However, only some 100 men per kilometre were left outside the forts, and the loss of the forward observation posts made fire control difficult.

On 19 June the forts in the extreme north-east suffered their first heavy air bombardment, but, apart from minor damage that could be rectified on the spot, nothing was put out of action. The lack of anti-aircraft guns made itself felt, though.

The following day the enemy troops who had earlier crossed the Rhine occupied the town of Haguenau. This was the rear base for the fortified sector, which was thus entirely surrounded. In spite of the armistice negotiations in progress, the guns continued to fire, causing heavy losses among the Germans who were trying to form up for a set-piece attack.

In the distant south Italy's attack had at last got off the ground. On 20 June they approached the frontier in the Alpine passes, but were repulsed with ease. The following day the attacks were repeated, mainly in the Mont Cenis and Modane areas. The French simply withdrew their forward positions, and the Italians ground to a halt under the accurate fire of the fortress artillery. During the next few days the attacks were repeated without any gains being made, and although the armistice was announced on the 25th, the main fort on the Mont Cenis position, the *ouvrage* La Turra, did not capitulate until 1 July. With its one turret containing a pair of 75s, it closed the pass entirely. The garrison was accorded the full honours of war by the astonished Italians, and French losses in the sector amounted to 4 killed, 21 wounded and 63 missing.[48]

Even further south an Italian attack along the Riviera coast was stopped by a French NCO with a handful of men in a bunker near Menton. However, the real 'tragicomedy' was being played out in the background. The Germans were in no hurry to clear the roads from the rear for their Italian allies and simply dragged their feet. Ciano, the Italian Foreign Minister, noted in his diary on 21 June that Mussolini felt cheated and humiliated, especially as the French had asked for an armistice. He felt that he would get nothing. On the evening of the 23rd French armistice delegates arrived in Rome. The fighting was almost over, but the 'victors' were still empty-handed. It was at this stage that a truly Machiavellian scheme was hatched, worthy of any Renaissance pope. Halder's diary tells the story. Apparently the Italians suggested that the Germans should transport some Italian troops by air via Munich to points in the rear of the French fortifications, so that they could justify claims to a slice of territory. Halder wrote, 'The whole thing is

German soldier guarding an entry block after the surrender. Note the damage to the *Cloche GFM* and the impact marks on the concrete

the cheapest kind of fraud. I have made it plain I will not have my name connected with that sort of trickery.' Later it was discovered that the plot had been initiated by a subordinate and the responsible chief-of-staff, Badoglio, disowned it. He was described by Halder as 'the only respectable soldier in the lot'.[49]

Among the forts in the north-east action continued. The handful of interval troops had been concentrated to defend the rear entrances and the turrets continued to fire. Schoenenbourg was subjected for the first time to a number of rounds from a 420 mm gun that the Germans had managed to emplace. This weapon was probably the sole survivor of the 'Big Berthas' that had pulverized the Belgian forts in 1914. One had certainly been retained at the Krupp test centre at Meppen, and it seems that this was packed into a large number of railway wagons and dragged all the way down to the Wissembourg area.[50] As a precaution, when this gun was firing, the turrets were lowered, but apart from enormous

99

craters, no damage was recorded. During the evening of the 22nd the Germans put on a display of pyrotechnics to celebrate the armistice that was to become effective at 00.35 hours on the 25th.

From then on German efforts at direct encroachment slowed down, although the forts continued to fire at anything that moved. Late in the evening of 24 June the Maginot Line was informed in a radio broadcast on the civilian network that they were to cease firing at 00.35 hours, but were to hold their positions and ignore enemy overtures. Only officially authorized representatives from GQG were to be received. One or two of the forts in the Metz RF continued to fire after the armistice, as they did not regard a civilian radio message to be a proper military order.

The guns may have ceased to fire but life still went on. German emissaries were politely turned away, while the garrisons set to work to clean up the accumulated mess left by weeks of fighting. In some forts the men were issued with new uniforms from stock, so that when they finally marched out they would present a smart appearance. According to Rodolphe, everybody was 'kept busy'. Adding up the score, they discovered that Hochwald and Schoenenbourg had fired a total of 38,116 rounds since the beginning of the war. Everyone assumed that under the terms of the armistice they would eventually be evacuated to the unoccupied zone, as they had not surrendered at the time of signing.

It was not until five days after the armistice had taken effect that representatives of General Weygand arrived in the Lauter RF to inform the garrisons that they were prisoners of war. Purely as justification, the Germans had insisted that as the forts were surrounded they would have had to surrender anyway. The French Government did not intervene on their behalf which was the cause of much justified ill-feeling. Thus, the following day they marched out for the last time on parade, being accorded the honours of war by the Germans. The local commanders on the spot genuinely regretted the fact that the men had to be made prisoner. The officers were permitted to retain their personal weapons.

As far as everyone was concerned the active life of the Maginot Line had ceased. However, there is no denying the fact that the old Verdun parole *on ne passe pas*, those evocative words from 1916, had been revived by the gallant men of the Maginot Line.

Chapter 12

1940–1944

After the garrisons had departed into captivity, certain officers and men were left behind to hand over the fortifications to the Germans. Inventories were taken and the forts minutely examined. All of a sudden the Maginot Line was all the rage. Setting the fashion, Hitler visited parts of the Line on 30 June, and he was followed by hordes of generals, other officers and journalists, all of whom were given guided tours. The visitors were transported as slowly as possible by internal railway, to increase the impression of size. One German officer described the interior of Hochwald as being as clean as a hospital, and several visitors dirtied their uniforms on the liberal coating of grease that had been applied to the guns. One report states that *Luftwaffe* officers openly wept when they saw that their bombs had made no impression at all. The upper surfaces of many of the forts were in direct contrast to the clinical interiors, being completely ploughed up by craters. The Germans simply could not believe, or did not want to believe, that the forts were still in working order.

Gradually the French personnel were relieved and sent away. Untrained Germans moved in, who proved incapable of maintaining the machinery, with the result that deterioration soon began to set in. They simply did not know what to do with the Maginot Line once they had got it. It soon lost its novelty value and was left to rot. Easily portable parts were removed for use in the Atlantic Wall defences, in the design of which Hitler himself took an active part. The very fact of the construction of this new continuous front would seem to prove that Hitler was impressed by the Maginot Line, in spite of his support for mobile warfare. He tried to build a bigger and better Maginot Line, which suffered from all the defects of the original, and which in turn was to prove ineffective.

As the Allied air offensive against strategic targets in Germany began to take effect, many of the Maginot *ouvrages* were turned into underground factories, mainly occupied with the production of war material.

It was not until October 1941, that any thought was given to the re-use of the Maginot Line as a defensive position in the event of an Allied invasion of the continent. In view of the fact that the works faced the wrong way and that it would cost too much to restore them, nothing was done at the time. However, the comment was made that certain parts could be used to block the roads leading towards the *Westwall*. In the late summer and autumn of 1944 some efforts were made to implement this plan and to rearm the sectors of Faulquemont and Wittring (the two flanks of the zone of inundations). This area was threatened by the advance of General Patton's 3rd US Army, which at

German troops outside the stores entry of a large fort. In this view the antenna is still in place

the time was stalled on the Moselle. So little attention had been paid to the works since 1940 that the German garrison commander at Metz had to apply to the army historical branch for a set of plans. However, the Americans were no better off, as they also had no plans. They had to round up a group of French engineer officers to provide drawings, which were hastily reproduced in the field.[51]

On 16 November, a few days before the fall of Metz, Hitler asked for information about the state of the Maginot Line, by which time the leading American units were already in the middle of it. There never was any co-ordinated plan to defend the position in 1944, but various retreating units, acting on local initiative, were able to impose delays on the Americans. The parts of the Metz RF to the west of the Moselle fell intact into American hands and were used subsequently as command posts and for training infantry to storm fortified positions.

The battle for Metz and the advance to the Saar started on 9 November, when the 90th Infantry Division crossed the Moselle at Cattenom to the north-east of Thionville, just opposite the point where the Maginot Line touched the river. A much older work (pre-1914 German), Fort Koenigsmacher, which was partly operational, severely hampered the crossing. This had been integrated into the Maginot system as a back-up position and re-equipped with French guns. Small groups of American troops had to fight their way on to the top and then subdue it by pouring petrol down the ventilation shafts, which they then lit by dropping thermite grenades. During the two-day battle they ran out of explosives and supplies had to be dropped to them from light aircraft.

From the Moselle the direction of the main advance was south-east, along the ridge into which the main position of the Maginot Line had been built. Many of the smaller shelters and casemates were occupied by the Germans, but these were ignored and left to be mopped up later. On 15 June, however, two battalions of the 357th Infantry Regiment came under accurate artillery fire as they approached the village of Budling. Shells landed at the rate of one per second, and it was discovered that they were coming from Block 8 of the Hackenberg *ouvrage*. This had been in use as a factory, but a group of Germans had managed to activate the block. It was of the casemate type and was armed with three 75 mm guns. A section of M10 tank destroyers opened fire on the casemate at a range of 2,750 m without success, and even heavy field artillery could make no impression. During the night two self-propelled 155 mm guns were moved up to within 2,000 m and managed to silence the

Block 8 at Hackenberg showing damage caused by American artillery in November 1944. This casemate block was originally fitted with three 75 mm guns

American troops in front of Block 8 at Hackenberg in November 1944, viewing damage caused by the 155 mm shells

casemate—one can still see the scars today. Apparently, the Americans were guided and advised by a certain Lieutenant Pinco who had actually served in Block 8 and had managed to avoid captivity in 1940. Before withdrawing the defenders exploded the remaining ammunition in the main magazine.[52]

During the night of 17/18 November the German 1st Army took up positions in the Faulquemont area. It is a paradox that an earlier 1st Army had been the one to attack the Maginot Line in exactly the same spot in 1940. Their successors were back in the same position but they were unable to maintain it for long. The Americans swept through in their particular form of *blitzkrieg*, leaving the bunkers to be blasted by the tank destroyers.

The other flank of the zone of inundations, to the east of the Saar, posed more of a problem. The Germans had occupied two of the *ouvrages* in the Wittrich-Achen area (Le Haut Poirier and Welshoff) where the *nouveaux front* joined the river. The Official Historian of the Campaign states, 'Actually these Maginot forts no longer presented any great tactical problem, although they appeared formidable enough to the assault teams sent against them.'[53] The American infantry used the same methods utilized by the Germans in 1940—a stealthy approach and then a rush to heave grenades and explosive charges in through the openings. Only the light weapons in the forts were manned, but these proved to have a high nuisance value, giving opportunities for gallantry on both sides. Welshoff was cleared fairly easily, but Le Haut Poirier put up a stiff fight. Owing to lack of Bangalore Torpedos there was difficulty in getting through the wire, and when the outer bunkers had been eliminated, there was still resistance from the centre of the fort. The Americans got to the rear of a block and tried to blast open the door with a tank destroyer. When this failed, they tried dynamite and, finally 200 lb of plastic explosive. This went off, blew in the door and detonated the ammunition inside, smearing the garrison all over the walls.

Had the Germans had sufficient troops available in the intervals and had they maintained the forts properly, it is probable that they could have imposed serious delays on the advancing Americans. However, the Maginot Line of 1944 was but a shadow of its former self.

Chapter 13

The Maginot Line today

After the war the Maginot Line was returned to its previous owners somewhat the worse for wear. Apart from the items removed from inside the forts themselves, the Germans had found the outside obstacle systems a useful source of scrap metal. Some of the forts had even been used for target practice. The French army immediately started to recondition the forts, over a period of 20 years, but in 1964 the decision was made to cease maintaining them. That year the authorities actually started to sell off small parts by public auction, and many of the purchasers came from neighbouring Germany. Since then many of the casemates and shelters have been transformed into holiday chalets, garages and mushroom farms, although the forts were all retained by the army. Many of them are still unapproachable as they are used for the storage of destructive military hardware.

As for the rest of it, it is simply still there, and presents a massive headache to the army who are responsible for keeping it safe. Wherever you go in north-eastern France along the frontier area, you cannot help but stumble over the remains. You can walk around on top of a fort without any idea of what is underneath. Turrets stick up from fields in which cows are grazing. In many areas the wire and the anti-tank rails can still be spotted.

Thanks to the initiative of a Major in the Engineers, the French army has restored the large Simserhof *ouvrage* which lies to the west of Lauter RF. This is used as a demonstration showplace and is in full working order. Indeed, it would be difficult to visit many of the deep forts unless the life support systems were functioning, owing to lack of ventilation.

Twin MG turret in the lowered position at the large Soetrich *ouvrage*

Apart from the army, certain enterprising individuals and bodies have already taken steps towards turning the Maginot Line into a tourist attraction. One Paris travel agency now runs weekend trips to the area, and an exhibition entitled 'Bunker Archaeology' was recently travelling around France.

One or two parts of the Line have come into municipal ownership and have been opened to the public. They include examples of most types of CORF structure, from the miniature to the magnificent. There is also an organization known as Amifort (*l'Association des Amis des Ouvrages Fortifiés de la région de Thionville*) which is devoted to the conservation of the works.

Near Entrange, which is a few kilometres to the west of Thionville, there is an example of the smallest type of work. This is the interval troop shelter at Zeiterholz, built to the rear of the main position. It is basically a two-storey bunker with two mixed-weapon turrets (automatic rifle and 50 mm mortar) on top. It was designed to house 100 men, was constructed between 1933 and 1934, and in 1940 was occupied by a part of the 169th Infantry Regiment. Entrusted to the care of Amifort, it houses a small museum of the weapons used in the Line—an 81 mm casemate mortar, a 47 mm anti-tank gun, standard automatic rifle, etc. One of the halls has been fitted out to show slides and one can also see the original beds and machinery.

Also in the vicinity, near the small town of Hettange Grande, there is the small *ouvrage* known as Immerhof, situated between the large forts of Soetrich and Molvange. It consists of an entry block and three infantry blocks with retractable turrets, one fitted with an 81 mm mortar and two with twinned machine-guns. The interior is in perfect condition and the *usine* is running during visits, producing power to operate the 81 mm turret that is demonstrated. As it was never attacked or even fired at, its condition has remained frozen in its 1940 state, even to the ladles hanging in their places in the kitchen. Visitors are given a tour, guided by members of the local volunteer fire brigade. This starts at the entry block where one can see the mechanism for changing from the machine-guns to the anti-tank gun in the firing chamber. One can also see the menacing embrasures of the interior blockhouse from which fire can be directed along the main gallery. From there, one is taken to the *usine*, hospital, barrack rooms and kitchens, before seeing the command post and the forward blocks. Finally, visitors are conducted to the mortar block where they can climb right up to the firing level. From there they emerge on to the surface via the emergency exit.

Right at the other end of the Maginot Line, near the village of Marckolsheim on the Rhine, one of the standard interval casemates, number 35/3, has been restored to its 1940 condition, when it briefly saw action on 15 June. It is fully equipped with its weapons, optical instruments and interior fittings, and is open every day during the summer.

The unfortunate La Ferté *ouvrage* has been transformed into a monument to those of the garrison who died there, and it too can be visited during the season. The Germans cleaned it up after they had captured it, but otherwise it has been left to show the craters.

Another fort that saw action was the small one at Bambesch which held out for several days during the attack on the Saar front. This is situated near the village of Bambiderstroff to the east of Thionville, and application to visit it should be made to the Mayor. This is an infantry work consisting of three blocks armed with a variety of light weapons.

A further example of the efforts of private individuals leading to the preservation of a fort is provided by the work numbered A2 and known as Fermont. This is at the extreme west of the main part of the Maginot Line and is situated just off the main road between Longwy and Longuyon. The association that runs it was given a concession by the military authorities in 1976. They found the fort in bad condition on account of the prevalent damp and a great amount of work has been required to put it back into working order. Apart from the usual two entry blocks there are seven infantry and artillery ones. Visitors are given a guided tour lasting two hours, part of which is made by internal

The memorial to those who died in the attack on La Ferté

A group of visitors seated on the waggons of the internal railway at Hackenberg. Note the power supply cables for the locomotive suspended from the ceiling (Kristensen)

railway. Fermont is open on Saturdays from October to March and every day during the summer.

Finally, there is the greatest fort of them all, Hackenberg, which is near the town of Veckring. This comes under the auspices of the Amifort organization who have managed to get most of it back into working order. Again the guided tour lasts some three hours, including transportation on the internal railway which runs for 3.2 km. All in all there are ten kilometres of tunnels in the fort. It is difficult to speak in superlatives, but a few details can perhaps give an impression of the size of the place. The deepest part of the fort, which covers a surface area of 160 hectares, is 96 m under the surface, and there are 515 steps from top to bottom. The casemate Block 8 required 5,000 cubic metres of concrete, and a turret for a pair of 75s, 280 tons of steel. The fort had 7 artillery blocks, 10 infantry ones and two entrances. The artillery comprised five 135 mm howitzers, four 81 mm mortars and nine 75 mm guns.

The guided tour starts at the stores entry block where there is a small museum of uniforms, plans and examples of the insignia worn by the fortress troops. From there the visitors are taken to the main magazine, the barrack area and the *usine*. Then the train takes one to the command post and the telephone exchange.

The next stop is at Block 9 which had weapons both in turrets and casemates. This involves a hefty climb from the counterweight level up to the firing chambers. One is then at ground level and can go outside to examine the upper surface. The visit ends with another train ride back to the rear entrance.

For full details of the visiting times for Zeiterholz, Immerhof and Hackenberg, one should write to: Syndicat d'Initiative, 1 Rue du Pont, F 47100 Thionville.

Whatever one may think about the purpose of the Maginot Line, the fact remains that it was an astounding feat of twentieth-century engineering, and its strictly functional architecture has a strange beauty all its own. It can never disappear, as to destroy it would require enough explosive to demolish a large part of north-eastern France. Thus it will remain, either as a curiosity or as a place of pilgrimage until its original purpose fades into oblivion. Then it will fall to the lot of future archaeologists to try to decipher the significance of the structures. Perhaps it will excite the curiosity of some twenty-fifth century Erich von Däniken.

Conclusion

In retrospect, the collapse of France in 1940 still continues to astonish the outside observer, but the reasons for this are beyond the scope of this study. However, the superficial reason for the defeat is often given as the 'Maginot mentality', and this has to be qualified. The original purpose of the Maginot Line was to eliminate the Franco-German frontier as a suitable area for a German attack, thus economizing on manpower and equipment which could then be reserved for a planned offensive or to counter-attack enemy penetration. We have seen the reasoning behind the construction, which was valid; it was a wise precaution to bar off as much of a long frontier as possible with fortifications, especially in view of the French demographic problem. Churchill said, 'Having regard to the disparity of the population of France to that of Germany, the Maginot Line must be regarded as a wise and prudent measure.'[54]

When it was being conceived and during the course of its construction, the panzer division had not been invented and mobile armoured warfare was but a dream. The whole basis of French strategy assumed an advance into Belgium with the active cooperation of that country, culminating in a conventional battle of attrition, ultimately with Anglo-American aid.

The French General Staff could hardly have foreseen the rise of Hitler during the 1920s, but they should have considered the possible defection of Belgium. When this happened in 1936 they were left out on a limb. It is clear that the Maginot Line could not have been extended to the Channel, for the reasons already stated, but the vital Ardennes area could and should have been more effectively fortified.

Fortification is essentially a passive entity and can do no more than support offensive action. Claudel uses the sword and shield simile—the sword is the striking weapon and the shield protects the striker. France had an excellent shield that covered part of the body, but the sword was missing. This was essentially where the fault lay. The only way to win a war is to destroy the enemy's forces, which pre-supposes an effective army of one's own. The French, however, believed that the offensive was unworthy of a peaceful people who had no claims against their neighbours. By pinning their hopes on a partial fortification they placed all their eggs in one basket, to the detriment of the field army. When the time came, the shield was there but the sword was blunt.

Propaganda is a subtle and invidious operative. There never was an official plan to deceive the French people and to lull them with a sense of false security; it just happened, and like Topsy, it grew. Where reality ended, the myth took over, creating the Maginot mentality that undoubtedly existed. What this all boils down to is that one cannot blame the fortifications for what happend to France in 1940; the fault lies in the use (or lack of it) that was made of them. The engineers charged with designing them produced a modern and satisfactory solution to the problems with which they were presented. Had they not been hampered by political and economic restrictions, they might well have come up with something even better.

The fact remains that had the Maginot Line, such as it was, been used properly, it could have altered the course of history on at least two occasions. Firstly, as a secure base for a vigorous offensive in the Rhineland in September 1939, and secondly, to back a counter-attack against the German columns moving through Luxembourg between 10 and 12 May 1940. Through the faults of its creators it never had the chance, and that is where the tragedy lies.

Appendix : Facts and Figures

These are taken from L. Claudel's book *La Ligne Maginot : Conception—Réalisation* and are quoted by kind permission of the owners of the copyright, the Association Saint Maurice.

Composition of the fronts

a North-eastern frontier and the Rhine;

23   artillery forts   ⎫
35   smaller infantry forts ⎬ a total of 36 blocks
                        ⎭

295   casemates and interval blockhouses
70   interval shelters
14   armoured interval observation posts
       plus a large number of minor fieldworks

b South-east frontier and Corsica:

23   artillery forts   ⎫
27   smaller infantry forts ⎬ a total of 146 blocks
                        ⎭

17   interval casemates (16 in Corsica, facing Sardinia)
3   interval observation posts
11   interval shelters
6   advanced post blockhouses
       plus 26 small advanced posts and 39 casemates built as field works

Weapons and armoured protection (CORF works only)

a Artillery

43   135 mm howitzers
132   81 mm mortars
169   75 mm guns of various types
———
344   pieces of ordnance (half in the north-east, half in the Alps)

b Armoured turrets

132 retractable turrets
1533 fixed turrets

Volume and cost

The system included more than 100 km of tunnels; 12 million cubic metres of earthworks; 1.5 million cubic metres of concrete; 150,000 tons of steel. 450 km of roads and railways (figures cited by General Tournoux). Starting with the law of January 1930 (2,900 million francs) plus the additional annual increments and work carried out by the army itself, one arrives at an estimated total expense of 5,000 million francs (1940 value).

For example :

A very large fort (Hackenberg) cost 172 million (1929–40)
A large fort (Simserhof, Molvange) cost between 70 and 80 million
A small fort (Aumetz) cost between 8 and 10 million
An interval casemate cost between 1.5 and 2.5 million
The above include land purchase and armament

Notes

As this is not an academic treatise, the notes have been kept to a minimum. However, the following references are offered to the reader who is in search of further information. Where only the author's name is mentioned, the title etc of the publication concerned will be found in the Bibliography.

1   For a concise summary see Shirer, p. 133 *et seq.*
2   Bouley, Section 3
3   Horne, A., *Verdun—the Price of Glory*, 1963
4   Claudel, p. 4
5   Debeney, p. 249
6   Quoted by Shirer, p. 192
7   Claudel, p. 4
8   For a discussion of the *couverture*, see Debeney
9   Clausewitz, *On War*, Vol. 2
10   For technical details of the Metz forts see, *Vierteljahreshefte fuer Pioniere*, 1936, Article by Major Dinter
11   Kemp, Anthony, *The Unknown Battle: Metz 1944*, To be published by Frederick Warne, London, 1981
12   Claudel, p. 7
13   Vitez, p. 73 and the OKW *Denkschrift*
14   Rodolphe, p. 54
15   Claudel, p. 24
16   ibid., p. 7
17   Rodolphe, p. 58
18   Claudel, p. 10
19   See various passages in the OKW *Denkschrift* on Czechoslovakia ·
20   Vitez, p. 128
21   Since writing this, a man whose opinions I trust, Herr Günther Fischer, informs me that he thinks the photographs were taken in the *Oder-Warthe Bogen* works. These were pre-war German defences built on the Polish frontier
22   The foregoing details are quoted by Telford Taylor
23   Horne, p. 24 *et seq.*

24 Eis, Egon, p. 162
25 Bouley, Section 1
26 Blumentritt, G. von, *Von Rundstedt—The Soldier and the Man*, London, 1952
27 Churchill, W. S., *The Gathering Storm*, p. 298
28 Detailed organization and fire control information in Rapin and Rodolphe
29 Vitez, p. 57
30 Rodolphe, p. 62
31 Quoted by Shirer, p. 194
32 Rodolphe, p. 72 *et seq.*
33 See article by Wanty, E.
34 Shirer, p. 606
35 Quoted by Horne, p. 95
36 Beaufré, p. 147
37 Bryant, A., *The Turn of the Tide*, London, 1957, p. 72
38 Beaufré, p. 39 *et seq.*
39 Taube, *Eisenbahngeschuetz Dora*, Stuttgart, 1979
40 For a resumé of the German war plans see Telford Taylor
41 See Horne, for the best general account of the Battle of France
42 Rodolphe, p. 85 *et seq.* The further references to operations in the Lauter RF are taken from this source
43 Guderian, *Panzer Leader*, London, 1952, p. 57
44 Liddell-Hart, B., *The Rommel Papers* London, 1951
45 For the French and German versions, see Rocolle and Vitez respectively
46 See Telford Taylor for second phase German planning
47 Article by Golaz
48 Rapin J-J., *A propos de la bataille des Alpes de Juin 40*, Revue Militaire Suisse, Sept 1977
49 Quoted by Telford Taylor
50 Rodolphe calculated the calibre by measuring shell fragments, and the presence of the gun is confirmed by the OKW *Denkschrift*
51 See Cole, *The Unknown Battle : Metz 1944*, op. cit., and 90th US Div. After Action Report
52 Gamelin, Paul, *La Ligne Maginot*, p. 5
53 Cole, p. 538
54 Churchill, op. cit., p. 373

Bibliography

Books

ANON, *The Maginot Line: The facts revealed by a French Officer*, London, 1939

ANON, *Unbezwinglicher Westwall*, Wiesbaden, 1940

ANTHERIEU, E., *Grandeur et sacrifice de la Ligne Maginot*, Paris, 1962

BEAUFRÉ, General A., *1940, The fall of France*, London, 1967

BELPERRON, P., *Maginot of the Line*, Paris, 1940

BOULEY, Gen., *Trois fortifications*, Restricted publication, 1953

BOURCIER, E., *L'attaque de la Ligne Maginot*, Paris, 1940

BRUGE, R., *Faites sauter le Ligne Maginot*, Paris, 1973   *On a livré la Ligne Maginot*, Paris, 1975   *Hitler attaque sur la Rhin*, Paris, 1976

BRYANT, A., *The Turn of the Tide*, London, 1957

CHURCHILL, W. S., *The Second World War*, Vol. 1, London, 1948

CLAUDEL, L., *La Ligne Maginot. Conception—Realisation*, Lavey (Switzerland), 1974, (privately published)

COLE, H. M., *The Lorraine Campaign*, (US Official History Series), Washington, 1950

EARLE, E. M. (ed), *Makers of Modern Strategy*, Princeton, 1945

EASTWOOD, J., *The Maginot and Siegfried Lines: Walls of Death*, London, 1939

GAMELIN, P., *La Ligne Maginot: Ouvrages de la région de Thionville*, Nantes, 1977
    La Ligne Maginot: Images d'hier et d'aujourd hui, Paris, 1979

GORCE, P-M. de la, *The French Army*, London, 1963

HORNE, A., *To Lose a Battle: France 1940*, London, 1969

HUGHES, J. M., *To the Maginot Line: The politics of French military preparation in the 1920s*, Cambridge Mass, 1971

KÜHNE, R. T., *Der Westwall*, Berlin, 1939

MAGINOT, Mdme M. *The biography of André Maginot: He might have saved France*, New York, 1941

MALLORY, K. and OTTAR, A., *The Architecture of War*, New York, 1973

MARY J. Y., *La Ligne Maginot*, Metz, 1980, (privately published)

NÉRÉ, J., *The foreign policy of France from 1914 to 1945*, London, 1975

PÖCHLINGER, J., *Das Buch vom Westwall*, Berlin, 1940

POL, H., *The Suicide of a Democracy*, New York, 1940

PRÉTELAT, Général A., *Le destin tragique de la Ligne Maginot*, Paris, 1950

RAPIN, Major J-J., *Une organisation exemplaire: l'artillerie des ouvrages de la Ligne Maginot*, Lavey (Switzerland), 1977, (privately published)

ROCOLLE, Colonel P., *Le Beton a-t-il trahi?* Paris, 1950

2000 ans de la fortification Française, Paris, 1974

RODOLPHE, Colonel R., *Combats dans la Ligne Maginot*, New ed, Vevey (Switzerland), 1973

ROWE, V., *The Great Wall of France*, London, 1959

SHIRER, W., *The collapse of the Third Republic*, London, 1970

TAYLOR, T., *The March of Conquest*, London, 1959

TOURNOUX, General P., *Haute Commandement: Gouvernement et défense des frontières du nord et de l'est, 1919–1939*, Paris, 1960

VITEZ, General L., *Ruhm und Fall der Maginot Linie*, Prague, 1942

WATT, D. C., *Too serious a business*, London, 1975

Articles

DEBENEY, Général M. E., *Nos fortifications du nord-est.*, Revue des Deux Mondes, September 1934

DEBENEY, Général M. E., *Le problème de la couverture*, Revue des Deux Mondes, 1938

GOLAZ, A., *L'offensive Allemande en Alsace de Juin 1940*, Rev. Hist. Armée, (no 3) 1963

GOYET, Lt.-Col. le, *La percée de Sedan en Mai 1940*, Rev. Hist. de la deuxieme guerre mondiale, July 1965

KEMP, A. G., *The Maginot Line today*, Fort (the journal of the Fortress Study Group), no 2, 1976

PAKENHAM-WALSH, Maj-Gen. R. P., *The Pill-Box row*, Royal Engineers Journal, 1960

PERRIN, Col. A., *L'artillerie d'ouvrage en première ligne*, Rev. Militaire Suisse, Sept 1978

ROUX, Commandant R., *Les dix mille du secteur fortifie de Faulquemont*, Rev. Hist. Armée, no 1, 1953

TOURNOUX, Général P., *Les origines de la Ligne Maginot*, Rev. Hist. de la deuxieme guerre mondiale, January 1959

WANTY, E., *La défense des Ardennes en 1940*, Rev. Hist. de la deuxieme guerre mondiale, April 1961

Documentary Sources

Denkschrift ueber die tschecho-slowakische Landesbefestigung. Oberkommando des Heeres. Berlin. 1941

Denkschrift ueber die Franzoesische Landesbefestigung. Oberkommando des Heeres. Berlin. 1941

Index

Index

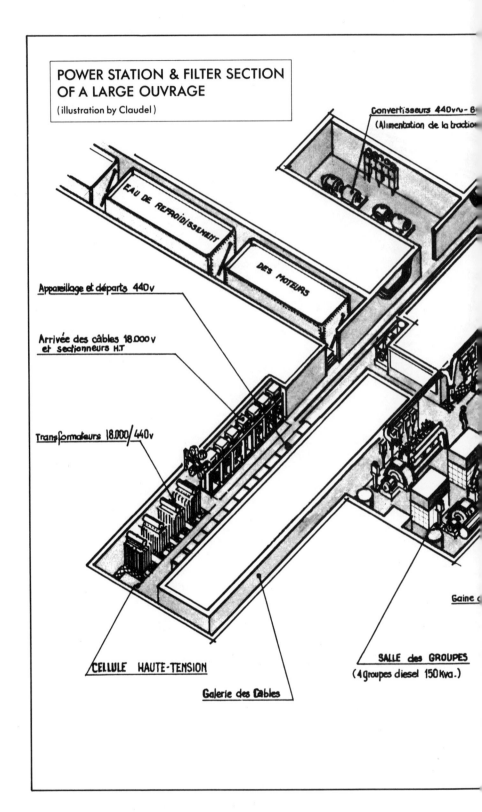

POWER STATION & FILTER SECTION OF A LARGE OUVRAGE

(illustration by Claudel)

Convertisseurs 440v∿ - 6
(Alimentation de la traction

EAU DE REFROIDISSEMENT

DES MOTEURS

Appareillage et départs 440v

Arrivée des câbles 18.000 v
et sectionneurs H.T

Transformateurs 18.000/440v

Gaine d

CELLULE HAUTE-TENSION

Galerie des Câbles

SALLE des GROUPES
(4 groupes diesel 150 Kva.)

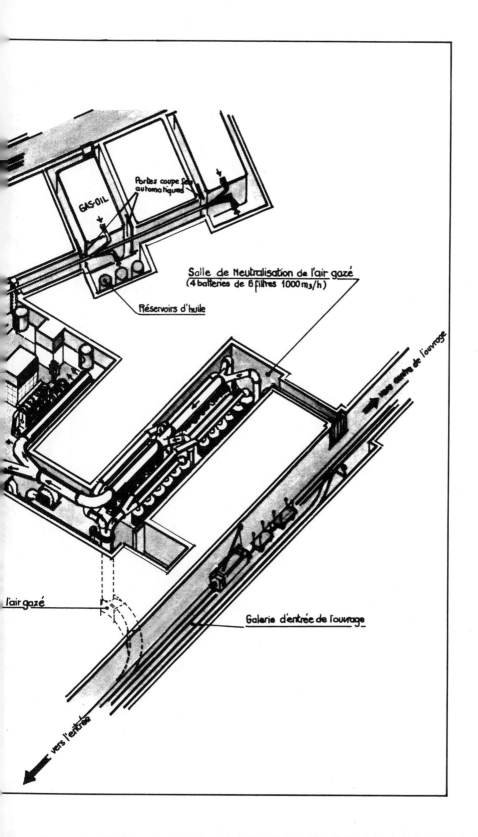

Portes coupe feu
automatiques

GAS-OIL

Salle de Neutralisation de l'air gazé
(4 batteries de 6 filtres 1000 m₃/h)

Réservoirs d'huile

vers centre de l'ouvrage

l'air gazé

Galerie d'entrée de l'ouvrage

vers l'entrée